Praise for The Art of Self-Leadership

Did you know you are capable beyond your imagining? — Heartfelt inspiration designed for the reader to be able to implement each and every concept. This is more than a book; it is a mentor.

Deeply personal, Bouhia shares her own journey, hard fought lessons, that now have served so many. In this book she shares a spiritual, personal and professional Codex to tap into your most potent self and to do so with gentle ease.

— Sierra Melcher, Founder of Red Thread Publishing and author of *Typo: The Art of Imperfect Creation* and many more

"If this beautiful book has found you, then you, dear reader, are being called to leadership. Your gifts are needed in this world, and it's time to step into your authentic authority and start putting them to good use. But don't panic; you're in the best of hands! Dr. Hynd's leadership codes will elevate you to greatness with more peace, ease, and joy than you ever imagined possible. Prepare to attract only love, respect, and magic money from here on out!"

— Dr. Adrienne MacIain, author of the bestselling series *Creative Living for All*

Hynd, you have created a very inspiring book! Your years of study and personal development show on every page. This is a true gift to the world. My hope is that it is read by millions and creates a legion of new wise leaders and successful entrepreneurs.

— Mimi Rich, Marriage and Family Therapist

Please leave your messages, comments, and appreciation for this book and our work on Amazon, Barnes & Noble, or Social Media. It would mean so much to me.

THE ART OF SELF-LEADERSHIP

12 CODES TO ELEVATE YOURSELF TO GREATNESS

DR. HYND BOUHIA

Red Thread Publishing LLC. 2024

Write to info@redthreadbooks.com if you are interested in publishing with Red Thread Publishing. Learn more about publications or foreign rights acquisitions of our catalog of books: www.redthreadbooks.com

Paperback ISBN: 979-8-89294-022-1

Ebook ISBN: 978-1-955683-90-6

Cover Design: BAL Method sas

CONTENTS

Dedicated to you, my beautiful Reader,

A culmination of four years of self-development and elevation,

my gift to you, sealed with love.

Thank you for being in my life.

Dr. Hynd

FOREWORD

You may not know who Hynd Bouhia is, but you should. Born in Morocco, when women were not encouraged to pursue an education abroad, she distinguished herself enough to get admitted into the Paris School of Engineering Centrale and earn a degree in industrial engineering. As a result of her work there, she distinguished herself yet again to the point of being actively recruited by her school's dean, going to her house and petitioning her family to allow her to enroll in the Paris-based engineering program in 1990s Centrale Paris. She then pursued her studies further with a PhD program at Harvard University.

Upon her arrival at Harvard, her mentor was surprised to learn that she was a woman with a degree from this country and an interest in science. After graduating, she got a position at the World Bank for eight years, where she worked and traveled to developing countries, creating plans for sustainability, economics, and improvement in the lives of women, children, and the environment.

The pressure from her family to get married and settle down raised many questions, prompting her to quickly exit her prestigious career, sell her waterfront Georgetown apartment, and return home. The

Prime Minister of Morocco invited her to work with him, and she later took a seat on the Casablanca Stock Exchange. Forbes nominated her as one of the 100 Most Influential Women in the World and among the top 100 Arab Women in Business. She has repeatedly petitioned to speak at international conferences.

She is a champion of women, STEM, and empowering women in Africa and the Arab World through the sciences, leadership, etc. She is also a mother of four children. She has been an author and respected member of several organizations since leaving the World Bank, and since the change in her career, she has started her own business. She faced several challenges, including when everything collapsed, which called for a solid resilience to face the resulting personal crisis.

She has built a new career, working with some of the most prestigious women in a mastermind course. To achieve incredible results, she had to face her demons and rebuild her life from the ground up, internally and professionally.

She has been published in English and French several times. Through a set of experiences ranging from great successes to painful failures, she created the 12 Codes of Self-leadership shared in this book.. Her mastermind class revolves around a three-part methodology she shared in her previous book, Believe, Act, Lead, which the 12 Codes of Self-Leadership in this book echo.

In many ways, this book is the next step from her book Believe, Act, Lead. However, it stands independently and offers transformational guidance for women seeking personal revelations and professional elevation. One of the critical mistakes in much of the leadership doctrine thus far is separating your personal and professional growth and goals. This book is a fluid unification that draws clear connections about how personal success and development and professional success and growth, rather than opposites completely separate, are more like an infinite loop. What goes on in one part of your life that goes and ripples in another? Through these 12 codes of self-leadership, you will learn more about

Hynd, who she is, and what her mark has meant for the world, but she also shares how you can apply these 12 codes to yourself for your elevation to greatness.

Genetically, financially, and personally, this book is a gift, a primer, a codex, an invitation to you if you hear the calling to become more intimately acquainted with yourself and fully step into who you can become. It is also a guide for how to implement your gifts for the betterment of the world.

INTRODUCTION

Dear Reader,

You are a woman in business: an entrepreneur, a leader in the corporate world, or making a difference on the local scale—your life and work matter. Like so many of us, you have experienced wins and faced setbacks. But if this book is in your hands, it is because you hope there is still more to come and that you have more to offer.

As I rebuilt from devastating corporate and financial loss, I discovered a method and core lessons that helped me grow intellectually and emotionally, allowing me to return to the impactful role I was meant for. I needed to share these lessons, and for the past few years, I have been doing so in my coaching and mastermind community. In this space, I support hundreds of women worldwide in rising to new heights, both in their careers and personal lives, by teaching and applying these codes.

The world is changing, but we still have much to do. In a world where leadership knows no boundaries, women increasingly take center stage on the global platform. Arguably, what the world needs more of is Feminine leadership. However, obstacles still entangle women and slow down our personal progress and collective influence.

The vast majority of literature available is written by men, for men.

There is value there, but something is still missing. As leaders, women need something different to complement the predominant leadership paradigm. These 12 Codes help you discover the leader within, reassert your greatness energetically and emotionally, and then apply it in the physical world.

These pages will cover a great deal of spirituality and energy. At first glance, this might seem different from leadership. It is rare in this genre, but the world needs your voice, heart, passion, and presence at the table to guide the fundamental decisions and direction as we step into the future.

We start within and work our way back out, in order to build the resilience and fortitude to hold our own leadership and to stay strong despite the circumstances.

BELIEVE ACT LEAD METHOD (BAL)

The BAL Method is the Framework for the 12 codes of self-leadership. When I started my mastermind, I designed the BAL method to focus our efforts. The 12 codes I share in this book take that method to the next level as we dig into the structure of how to apply this to your own life.

1. The first step of the **Believe, Act, Lead Method** starts with *Believing* in yourself, the possibilities, and your capacity to attract everything in your life and all the potentialities when you access the field of energetics and miracles.
2. The second step is to *Act On It* and reverse-engineer the whole scheme to achieve the goals of acquiring knowledge, mastering leadership skills, and making excellence your brand.
3. The third step is *Leading* and opening the channel to abundance and prosperity.

These three steps comprise the sections of this book. My book *Believe*

Act Lead* fully describes the method, which became an overnight best-seller. Your journey to creating wealth, success, and impact begins here. These twelve codes are a way to unveil the perfect diamond inside of you, taking off the covering layers one by one so that it shines brighter than ever.

Lead yourself

Lead your family

Lead your team

Lead the world

My Story

I held a high-powered job, traveling to exotic places and advising on critical development issues. Then I felt a calling to return home to Morocco, primarily pressured by my family as the clock was ticking and it was time to settle down and start a family. So, I left my influential high-earning position at the World Bank. I returned to my home country, Morocco, to work for the Prime Minister–a prestigious place to start a new chapter in my career. Then, I was appointed Managing Director of the Casablanca Stock Exchange, and later on, I started my own business.

I had built my little empire, my children were still young, and I was making a difference in the world. I had everything that any successful aspiring woman could want.

Through a series of unfortunate events, I was in corporate bankruptcy and crawled into a hole. I was afraid to answer the phone; I tried to disappear as it felt like a nightmare.

It has taken me three years to admit as much, but I have learned much in that time. I have rebuilt myself, learning elemental lessons, and I have also been fortunate enough to rebuild a community to teach hundreds of international executives worldwide what I have learned.

I share my personal stories, trials, and triumphs in these pages. Some of the women in my mastermind have graciously allowed me to share bits of their stories. We will explore spiritual and energetic themes and

---

*   https://www.amazon.com/dp/B0BKGW1667

practical, applicable tools for building greatness from within to elevate your leadership game.

Many believe spirituality, love, and energy do not belong in business. I disagree. Let me show you why. I intend these codes to become tools for charting your path towards greatness.

This book provides the tools to shatter the glass ceiling, break free from self-doubt, and lead with unwavering confidence. By the time you finish reading it, you'll have become an icon of leadership who inspires, empowers, and elevates those around you while advocating for positive change.

Leading is an Art

IT STARTS FROM WITHIN

The lessons in this book have been in the making for four years. That is approximately 10,000 hours of contemplation, studying, and understanding the depth of what it means to lead. Malcolm Gladwell's 10,000-hour rule states that it is the time required to master a subject. I do not pretend to have mastered the topic yet, but I know that leading starts within, and then the rest follows. Let me save you some time and share what I have learned.

As I write, I am on track again in my entrepreneurship journey, which started almost a decade ago. I structured and closed multiple million-dollar projects as a strategist, advisor, and investment manager. After stumbling, I found the courage and self-help to stand back up. We often say that reaching rock bottom means changing directions. But this can only happen if you can access your inner strength and ignite your spark.

I did it!

I returned from the most profound setback and have shown others how to do it. I want to celebrate with you by sharing all the codes I received and channeled through these three years. Recognize that you are becoming planted when you feel buried in the darkest hole and face the most challenging circumstances. The wisdom you gain from the lessons learned makes the soil more fertile. Even when it seems like nothing is happening, trust that miracles are forming in the darkness, and new life will emerge from there.

WHERE SCIENCE AND SPIRIT COME TOGETHER

As an engineer and a mathematician, I have built a logic sequence in my mind over the years. I relied on science and my understanding of everything around me as a professional, a mother, and a woman. I followed the dominant leadership narrative, which only got me so far.

As I deepened my understanding of the power of the mind and the secret behind a life of happiness and abundance, I realized that it is beyond logic and science. There is a dimension that we keep under the radar. On the one hand, as an educated person trained in the scientific paradigm, I find it hard to perceive. On the other hand, as a spiritual person, I learned how to perceive infinite power, universal intelligence, and the divine to ignite my strength. It was not about external knowledge; it was about the inner game. The profound understanding of who I am inside, what drives and affects me, and what controls my emotional intelligence.

My personal and professional crisis was a gift. It allowed me to spend three, almost four years now, with intentional discipline and resilience. As I look back, I am proud of the woman I am, the one who not only did not give up on herself when everyone else had but also elevated women to rise and be reborn like phoenixes from the ashes.

> *I found* love *within me and started to magnetize more of it into my life from everywhere.*
> *I found* peace *within me and made it my mission for the world.*
> *I found* infinite abundance *within me and understood how to connect with the portal of* money and prosperity.

*I found myself leading again in my family, community,
and globally.*

MAKE THE CODES YOUR OWN

My ultimate goal has been to spread the secret about how you can be in charge of yourself. Your life is yours to create and shape. The twelve codes are a roadmap, an effortless step-by-step transfer of wisdom and understanding you can shape as best fits your lifestyle and aspirations.

The codes of this book are about the art of leading yourself so that you become the best human expression of the purity of your soul. There is a divine perfection inside you, me, and all of us; the secret is to tap into it.

No one could ever provide a done-for-you scheme to build your legacy. By its very definition, life is yours to make. *But* these codes will help you align with a shape that structures your mind and spirit. A shape I built for myself using mathematical and musical logic.

You will find *an* interconnection between the mind, body, and soul. Let's navigate together through the concepts and codes one by one. I want them to build a stronger you that becomes undeniably powerful to take on the world. Consider this your guide and my gift to you, given with all my love. Ready to fill your heart with the love that you deserve?

A voyage inside you helps you reconnect with emotions and feelings that may have been left unprocessed for many years, creating a wound or an uncleared blockage. As I am taking you through my process, I aim to ignite similar discoveries and reconnections with the wealth of hidden talent and creativity you have inside.

My dream is a world where we love each other honestly and understand that we are the only ones in charge of turning our desires into reality. There will be more peace, more empathy, and more care. Smile at life, and life will smile back at you.

Enjoy reading it and sharing it with your dearest ones. Let's change the world together, bringing love, peace, and excellence to every service we provide to humanity. It's about leading yourself first so you can lead the world.

Together, we make a difference.

Together, we spread love and peace.

Together, we change the world.

PART ONE
BELIEVE

Believe in yourself.
Believe in the possibilities.
Believe in humanity.
Believe in miracles.
Believe in magic.
Believe in love.

Marvel at the depth of each one of us as you master your emotional intelligence. Each of us is capable beyond our imagining, but *you are correct if you believe* yourself to be the victim or stuck because you are only as capable as you think yourself to be. *If you believe* your abilities to be limitless, then anything is possible.

In Part One, we explore the first four codes designed to enhance your capacity to believe in yourself.

CODE 1 – THE MAGIC OF GRATITUDE
CODE 2 – THE GIFT OF FORGIVENESS
CODE 3 – THE POWER OF LOVE
CODE 4 – THE FORCE OF LIFE

Explore your capacity to believe in these first four codes. While reading them, open your eyes wide to notice the universe and its depth by infusing the magic of gratitude, welcoming the gift of forgiveness while nurturing the power of love, and holding on to the force of life.

There is so much depth in the universe and power in the infinite intelligence.

We can only really grasp some things, even if we go deep in our contemplation and understanding. Even in the depths of our being, there is always more to see than we can imagine.

You can wait for something that makes you smile, but you will be waiting forever. Or you can choose to start smiling on your own. The universe will inevitably follow.

You can call yourself the inevitable millionaire. When you put your mind to becoming a happy multi-millionaire, you align with that.

As you read this book, remember that you are the ONE to lead yourself through the changes to bring about the life you desire: setting up long-term objectives, visualizing your goal-achieved self, and making the decision to turn your life around starts with BELIEVING and encompasses the starting point.

Rock Bottom (Back Story)

I couldn't bear the sound of the phone ringing while everyone focused on my struggling business. Although I prayed and wished for a miracle, I felt powerless to stop it. The situation was too complicated and intertwined with many issues beyond my control to save the business.

Each time the phone rang, I was startled. My heart started beating, and heat rushed to my head—everything was aching in my body.

I was scared and stressed and just wanted to hide and let the nightmare go away.

I wanted time to stop and swallow me. I will return from it when everything is cleared and becomes normal. A professional crisis–a corporate bankruptcy- could be more heavy and painful than anyone could imagine when you have given your job everything you've got. But I could not do that to my children; my daughters looked at me as their role model. I had to be there for them, but how?

Ten years ago, I embarked on my entrepreneurial journey in May 2014; I was ready to fly independently and build a legacy. I launched my first company for strategic advisory and consultancy and then grew to create more sophisticated corporations for advanced financial structuring and investment mechanisms. The team grew with the activities, and we made a referenced multiple 7-figure brand around impact investment and sustainable finance. However, the stress and the pressure heightened, and I found myself amid betrayal, losses, and several dilemmas to face on my own as a manager and the group leader. It was a nightmare I had feared for as long as I could remember during my professional life.

Leadership is not just about the wins. It is about how we show up in the struggles. Even when it felt like my world and my life were collapsing around me, I got through by returning to Gratitude. Sometimes, what we fear the most happens, just as if we were attracted to it. I understood this is not a punishment from the universe but a rite of passage to free ourselves from that fear.

I am standing as proof of these concepts from my own life and those of women I worked with inside our mentorship programs. Everything has limitations except the power of the divine, the more significant force —or what you see as the infinite intelligence—and the connection you can create from within. There is perfection inside you and endless light when we can tap into it. You become a magnet as you walk into any room and any space. That magnetism draws people to you and raises you to the frequency of wealth, success, joy, happiness, good health, and love time, *and* you keep a vision in your heart that permits you to dream freely. You can have it all. There is nothing that creates limitations or constraints but our own beliefs, blockages, and self-sabotaging attitude. Start with remembering all you have to be grateful for.

CODE 1
THE MAGIC OF GRATITUDE

How can you lead yourself when you don't appreciate all you carry inside of you?

Absolutely impossible.

There is incredible power in gratitude, so we start here. Your Beliefs create your reality.

Count what is going right. Count all you have to celebrate. Make it a habit, and you will draw more of what you are grateful for.

Not only does this work in refocusing your mindset and rewiring your brain, but it energetically calls forward what you desire. Neuroplasticity is becoming a widely accepted and understood concept that whatever is repeated shapes the brain's physiology, creating more connections and ease. "What you focus on expands" suggests that our attention and intention significantly shape our experiences and reality.

So you either harness the power of your focus to enhance and accelerate your inner greatness, or that same attention can drag you down, focusing on all that you haven't accomplished, all the ways you have failed, and all that has not worked in your favor.

Whether you prefer the neuroscience explanation, the spiritual way, or the laws of attraction interpretation, the story is the same.

Gratitude should become a habit—redirecting your thoughts toward everything in your favor. First thing in the morning, as you open your eyes, direct your attention to gratitude for the miracle of life, for the bed you find yourself in, and for your capacity to breathe and feel the warmth of the sun on your cheeks—gratitude for loved ones who are with you and those who think of you.

Deep appreciation involves being *emotionally connected* to what you already have and who you are. Acknowledge the privilege you have; millions of people around the globe live on less than one dollar a day. If you are holding this book, you are not one of them.

Quickly, time, *and* we take things for granted when we lose track of the fundamentals. Everything seems meaningless when we focus on *the lack of money, time, and love.* We quickly shift to an energy of scarcity, translated into a frequency of lack and vibrating as such in the universe. Negativity bias is what neuroscientists refer to as the habitual focus on the negative. The mind puts roughly ten times the focus on adverse circumstances as positive ones. Not only does this create a perception of scarcity, but it also draws scarcity, doubt, and fear. We need to intentionally counteract this by redirecting our thoughts to gratitude.

Having studied physics early on and delved into the world of energy, I've always been intrigued by this quote: "Everything is energy, and that's all there is to it. Match the frequency of the reality you want, and you cannot help but get that reality. It can be no other way. This is not philosophy. This is physics." While the source of this quote is uncertain, it is often attributed to Albert Einstein's theories. (We dive more into this in the section about energetics.) However, throughout the book, the driving thread is that fine line between energetics and our capacity as humans to take action and implement a sound plan to improve our lives and be happy and fulfilled.

I didn't call it gratitude in my younger years, but the appreciation of life and our ability to help and give back shaped my upbringing. The obligation to do good and be pleasing to the people around us is part of both Moroccan and Tunisian cultures. Some people grow up with a beautiful taste of gratitude, and others carry bitterness by focusing on lack. The mindset you choose is up to you.

FILL YOURSELF WITH GRATITUDE

When you feel gratitude, you will stir your thoughts away from fear and worries. I know it sounds too easy to be true. I thought so, too, in the beginning. But, with discipline, meditation will calm your mind, and starting your day with thanks will make things shift from within.

You won't notice that shift immediately. Stick with it anyway—initially, a forced discipline or a strong intentionality might be the only way to integrate it into a daily habit. Eventually, it starts becoming a habit, and you begin to notice how your thoughts turn into something solid—becoming law. You do what you say you will do. That feeling is beyond the recognition of it all. Feeling appreciation itself becomes something to be grateful for. It all starts to compound on itself. The impact is beyond what anyone could imagine. I invite you to make it your new lifestyle.

Every day is a new opportunity, a new chance to help yourself move forward and create something new. When you start appreciating the delicateness of those unnoticed moments, you will begin to absorb the happiness from gratitude, love, and care for yourself.

We rush through our days. If we were to sit and remember what we did, we would have forgotten a big part of it already because we go through the day ticking different boxes, one after the other. We get lost in a busy schedule, a busy life, and a busy mind. We leave no space for contemplation.

Feeling the present moment brings you joy—and the very exercise of gratitude and appreciation is a way to ground yourself in the present. Use all your senses and reconnect with yourself in that moment and place.

Finding Gratitude, Everywhere

I followed my inner calling this year. I found myself traveling through places where I grew up. I encountered and entertained the most beautiful emotions of joy, laughter, love, happiness, and fulfillment.

It took me back to my mother's town and our childhood summer house in Tunisia, traveling through the sweet and soft feeling of freedom and unconditional love. Later, as I returned to each place, I returned to my dorm in Harvard Yard.

In Tunisia, my happy childhood summer place, I reawakened a spark that felt like fireworks inside me while being grounded.

Returning to this place reminded me of so much of the magic of growing up: the child's feeling of safety in my grandma's arms, the excitement of love at first sight, the sweetness of innocent laughter, laughing about everything and nothing, walking for hours on the top of the rocks, collecting small fish and crabs and throwing them back into the water.

Gratitude Makes Magic

I had the dream to go to Harvard. I remember one night, lying on the sand in the summertime, my sisters and I watched the stars, and I made a wish. We loved doing that—it connected us to the universe and cosmic power. It makes me smile thinking about it now. Look at the stars and make a wish. It's basic and straightforward. I wished and believed with childhood enthusiasm. Two years later, I was preparing to settle in Perkins Hall at Harvard University. Two years earlier, the dean of the pre-engineering school had come to my home in Casablanca to convince my parents to let me study abroad. That was magic. I believed in myself enough to dream the impossible into being possible.

Grateful for all my opportunities, I dedicated myself even more to studying. Determined to return to my country and contribute, I knew my story wasn't just for me. It was for every young girl who doubted that achieving her dreams was possible and for those who lacked the opportunities I was blessed with.

I wanted every young woman to have faith that something was

possible for her no matter what. There will be a guiding arm of fate on your path. There is invisible energy helping us when we genuinely believe and surrender to it. My guides and that "invisible arm of fate" were my professors. But what saved me, in reality, was my gratitude—I knew that the only way to break free from traditional constraints was to excel in school and make the most of every chance available.

I was so excited and bubbly on the first day I arrived at Harvard. I met my professor and thesis advisor, Peter Rogers. "I am your new student," I said. He was stunned. "You are actually a girl," he said. From my name, he couldn't tell. I was breaking the tradition already.

I felt part of magic every day—gratitude for everything I had brought more opportunity. I manifested magic.

GRATITUDE RIPPLES

I spent a month back in Cambridge, MA., this summer with my children.

It felt so good to be back strolling in the Harvard Yard–it felt like déjà vu. While my eldest participated in the Harvard Summer Program, my three daughters came with me everywhere.

The path before them is so different from when I was young. My dream has already come true.

Like years before, I was grateful for my opportunity to be there. I was truly blessed to sit across from world-class professors and experts in the front seat of world change and technology transfer, understanding and deepening all the knowledge I could acquire to grow as a strategist in sustainability and decision-making.

STRENGTHENING YOUR INNER GAME

For the past four years, I have focused on strengthening the inner game, understanding human behavior, and helping women in my community do the same. Inside our leadership and mentorship programs, women found the joy of life and fell in love with every part of who they were. Most importantly, they navigated the journey while celebrating success after success.

Things start to unfold when we reframe our mindset by remembering all we have to be grateful for and love every moment. I saw it repeatedly with women inside our Mastermind.

Case Study from the Global Mastermind Community

Ines, the president of a foundation for children's education in Croatia, put these codes to work for herself. She fell in love with life again. The exercise of morning gratitude did wonders for her behavior and emotional state. It inspired her to uplevel her branding, which then started attracting more funding and new partnerships for her foundation.

Gratitude opens the door to feeling whole and appreciative of a meaningful life. It is also the key to receiving love and abundance. It will happen as you keep yourself disciplined and remember to integrate a moment of acknowledgment into your day because discipline helps you stay on track and create new emotional habits, ultimately creating a powerful feeling of being full and fulfilled—a state of Nirvana.

When you try it, you can see the incredible unfolding in front of your eyes. Then, use it again to see how it compounds more things for which to be grateful.

Look around and see how much harmony there is. Feel the present moment. The more intentional you are about feeling the present, the more you will attract situations for which you will be grateful.

So, take a moment to look around and appreciate what you see. Admire nature and connect with it. This practice is how you find harmony around you and create unforgettable moments.

You will experience incredible success and wealth manifesting through beautiful connections and relationships. Follow the codes one by one, and let the magic unfold in your life through these pages.

ACTIVITY FOR CODE 1

Your task for this code is to sprinkle some magic in your day. Integrate into your morning routine a gratitude list and connect with it emotionally.

The magic wand is in your hand, and the first move starts with a gratitude list. Write a list of 10 things you are grateful for now to practice. Then, make it a habit. Dedicate a notebook to gratitude and practice daily.

1.

2.

3.

4.

5.

6.

7.

8.

9.

10.

Introspection

I left my position at the World Bank to return to my hometown, Casablanca and serve in my own country. A promise I had given myself when I went to study abroad. A promise to acquire all the knowledge and learn how technology gets transferred so that countries advance, develop, and thrive. Nevertheless, I might have taken that decision way too fast for my adaptation, so it came with many regrets. I sold my apartment in such a rush because I might change my mind if I took too long. I needed to burn all the bridges this time to ensure I wouldn't return. Was it the right decision? Was it the right way of doing it?

For 15 years, I have beaten myself up for how and why I left and what I could have decided differently. This summer, I went back, having done the healing work of forgiveness, and could see it all anew for the gorgeous experience it was.

When we identify what we need to heal and untangle the emotions from the experience, we liberate ourselves from old stories of regret that hold us back.

I started at the World Bank as an intern in the summer of 1996, working in the Middle East and North Africa with Tony Garvey, a specialist in water strategies. I was ready to conquer the world, eradicate poverty, and be at the center of developmental initiatives for a better world. It was a dream! It was finding oneself where everything was happening. The World Bank was a lifestyle; I loved every part of it.

I was single, a high-level professional woman, jet-setting around the world, going to the airport every other week to go on a mission—and planning the next one before even finishing one.

On the plane and during long, sweet evenings, sitting in a tropical garden or by the sea somewhere in Thailand or Malaysia, I spent many hours thinking about the future: Would motherhood find its way into my busy and unconventional life? Would I ever marry? Would I rise as a professional or be closer to my family?

I had the world at my feet and my life ahead of me, but I chose to leave and return to my hometown. For years, I have regretted the decision of selling my Watergate apartment. I thought I made the wrong choice. My personal development was a long, slow process. Still, I felt liberated this summer because by returning, I forgave myself for my mistakes and the snap decisions influenced by fear, family pressure, and societal stereotypes. For years, I hated myself for how I left Washington. I could not make peace with it.

There was a long list of things I needed to forgive myself for. For so long, I didn't know where to start.

It was all triggered by the need to forgive myself for enduring corporate bankruptcy and the losses I had to absorb. I was so ashamed of all this happening and hurt by the succession of events that kept on coming. Then, when I touched that scary rock bottom, I had to rewire myself. Following the BAL method, piece by piece, and through these building blocks, forgiveness was essential.

I had to forgive myself and love myself back to find love again for that little girl in me who didn't know how. (Love comes next.) I had to forgive the woman in me who took on too much responsibility and the professional who wrapped herself in tough skin, but her own was too soft and cracked.

2023 is a significant date in this journey of forgiveness. That summer was one of returning to many old places.

Walking down the streets of Washington, D.C., brought so many memories.

You get to appreciate that over and over when you can forgive yourself for the past and things that didn't go how you wanted them to.

I had not returned to my apartment building and area for so many years! The reasons I left the Watergate apartment and resigned from my great job at the World Bank impacted my life significantly. Those reasons were primarily the clock ticking and family pressure to return home and settle down; I could not get myself to make peace with it. Not that I regret returning to Morocco, but I had many emotions that needed untangling but were left unprocessed. Each time I remembered, I felt a pinch in my heart—I should have planned differently and thought it through, but it kept going on, pulling me into a spiral of disappointment and bitterness.

I was clinging to a past that no longer existed and trying to make sense of it. I never thought of the need to talk about it, let alone to understand the emotional weight it was putting on me—but it felt heavy. If you wonder what invisible constraints mean, this is an example of an utterly invisible blockage that didn't make any sense yet was haunting me.

So much healing came with simply the act of forgiveness.

CODE 2
THE GIFT OF FORGIVENESS

C ode 2 is the most difficult to apply in your life and also the most liberating. There are ways to set yourself free through its mastery. Forgiving yourself and the past makes it easier to draw lessons and wisdom from the past, making you believe more in yourself and your ability to lead and create your best life.

How can you lead yourself when you carry bitterness inside?

At times, you might feel that revenge can set you free, and holding on to rage and grudges allows you to remember it forever. It doesn't; quite the opposite. This mentality fosters bitterness, pulling you down and keeping you in the same cycle. It also leads you to develop defense mechanisms that confine you to numerous constraints.

WHAT YOU RESIST, PERSISTS

Experts say it takes twenty-one days to change a thought. But when you have thousands of thoughts in a day, how many days will that be?

If you go to the gym once expecting to see results on your figure, you will be disappointed. Significant change requires more than one try.

Shifting a paradigm and changing a story in your subconscious mind are the same. Reprogramming old beliefs and thoughts anchored and repeated in your mind takes conscious effort and lots of repetition.

Walking back through the streets of Georgetown made me feel young again. I was grateful for the moment. I had forgiven myself for a choice I doubted. Returning to this place was the final step in my forgiveness journey. I dusted off any bitterness left and felt the sweetness of the place.

Almost twenty years have passed since I left my position as Senior Financial Officer at the World Bank. Until this summer, I could not return, always wondering if leaving was the right decision. I had to understand what forgiving oneself meant before letting go of the "what if" and embracing my journey as it is.

Forgiveness helped me find peace and feel joy and happiness in every step. So, I came back filled with gratitude rather than regret. It is incredible how a switch in the energetics made me feel free and empowered. I felt in charge again rather than carrying a story of loss.

Self-forgiveness can be a challenging but precious practice for personal growth and well-being. It involves releasing yourself from guilt, self-blame, and regret. Here are some strategies and tools to help you practice:

- **Self-Reflection:** Take the time to reflect on the situation or actions that require forgiveness. Understand the underlying reasons for your choices and behavior. Acknowledge that we all make mistakes and have imperfections, which are part of being human.
- **Accept Responsibility:** Understand the reasons behind your actions and take responsibility for them. Avoid self-victimization. Accepting responsibility is a crucial step in the self-forgiveness process.

- **Empathy for Yourself:** Treat yourself with the same compassion and empathy you would offer a friend in a similar situation. Understand that you, like everyone else, are fallible. Be kind and understanding to yourself.
- **Learn from Your Mistakes:** View your mistakes as opportunities for growth. Ask yourself what you can learn from the situation and how to prevent a similar mistake. This perspective shift can make the process of self-forgiveness more constructive.
- **Practice Self-Compassion:** Self-compassion involves treating yourself with the same kindness, care, and understanding you would offer to someone you love. Use self-compassionate, self-talk, affirmations, and reminders that you deserve forgiveness and healing.
- **Release Negative Emotions:** Engage in activities that help you release negative emotions associated with the situation. Activities include journaling, talking to a trusted friend or therapist, or physical activities like yoga or meditation.
- **Set Boundaries:** If the situation involves someone else, consider setting healthy boundaries to protect yourself from further harm, including distancing yourself from toxic relationships or communicating your boundaries.
- **Mindfulness and Meditation:** Mindfulness practices can help you stay focused on the present moment and avoid ruminating on past mistakes. Meditation can also promote self-compassion and self-forgiveness by allowing you to focus on positive intentions.
- **Seek Support:** Sometimes, seeking support from a therapist or counselor who can guide you through self-forgiveness is helpful. They can provide tools and techniques tailored to your specific needs.
- **Rituals or Symbolic Gestures:** Some people find solace in symbolic gestures like writing a forgiveness letter to themselves, lighting a candle, or performing a ritual that signifies their commitment to self-forgiveness.

- **Time and Patience:** Self-forgiveness is a process that takes time. Be patient with yourself and understand that it may not happen overnight. Revisit these strategies as needed and give yourself the time to heal.

Remember that self-forgiveness is a journey that may require ongoing effort. The goal is to free yourself from the weight of past mistakes and allow yourself to move forward with a greater sense of self-acceptance and inner peace.

When we are young, we worry about the future. When we are older, we think over every choice we make. *My younger self fixated on the question: If I have girls, how could I make it easier for them to go after their dreams and have a rewarding life away from stereotypes and heavy constraints?*

I have spent so much time and energy holding onto the past and second-guessing the choices made by my younger self. Forgiveness allows us to relax into trusting fate. Holding on to doubt is micro-managing the past.

Fast-forward, it all unfolds in the most beautiful way. I could never have planned or predicted it. We spend our time worrying about how to get what we want, thinking that we could craft it better than the universe, the divine.

The divine, the universe, will always create the best path for us—one that fits perfectly and unfolds little by little, piece by piece. Until the whole picture becomes clear, it's impossible to understand how everything synchronizes beautifully together fully.

Surrendering to the beauty of life means embracing this truth. The Code encourages you to invite more purity into your life, which begins with forgiving yourself and others. Doing so will deepen your understanding and release the ropes holding you back.

Take a moment and count back the fantastic things you have gone through in your life.

Focus on the little things you are proud of. Find happy moments and replay them in your mind. Revisit exciting feelings and plant them back in your heart. It will make you feel alive—anchor in positivity, dust off all the rest.

Negativity pulls you down. It blocks your capacity to manifest and listen to your intuition – your inner GPS. Forgiveness releases all that does not serve you anymore.

FORGIVENESS OF OTHERS

When you work in a team or manage a family, you inevitably interact with others, and there will be hurt sometimes. How well you navigate and manage your emotions and how skilled you are at forgiveness and communication will determine how you move through or get sidelined, but that hurts.

Forgiveness of others is a fundamental and significant aspect of human relationships, offering a powerful mechanism for healing, reconciliation, and personal growth. It is crucial to promote emotional and psychological well-being while fostering healthier connections. Here are several compelling reasons why forgiveness is so important:

- **Emotional Liberation:** Forgiveness frees individuals from the heavy burden of anger, resentment, and bitterness. Holding onto grudges can take a toll on one's mental health, leading to stress, anxiety, and even depression. When we forgive, we release these negative emotions, allowing for positive feelings like peace and contentment.
- **Relationship Repair:** Forgiveness is often the cornerstone of rebuilding fractured relationships. It opens the door to communication and understanding, allowing for reconciliation and the restoration of trust. It can lead to more harmonious and productive interactions in personal and professional settings.
- **Personal Growth:** Forgiveness is a powerful tool for personal growth and self-improvement. It requires individuals to reflect on their emotions, empathize with the offender, and find strength in their ability to move forward. This self-awareness and resilience can lead to

increased self-esteem and a deeper understanding of one's values.

- **Physical Health Benefits:** Studies have shown that forgiveness can positively impact physical health. Lower stress levels associated with forgiveness can reduce the risk of heart disease, improve the immune system, and lead to better sleep. Thus, it's a psychological benefit and a boost for one's overall well-being.
- **Cultural and Societal Harmony:** On a broader scale, forgiveness contributes to healing communities and societies plagued by conflict and injustice. Acts of forgiveness can pave the way for reconciliation, peace, and social cohesion, as seen in various instances of post-conflict forgiveness and reconciliation processes worldwide.
- **Spiritual and Philosophical Significance:** Many religious and philosophical traditions emphasize the importance of forgiveness as a virtue. It provides a way to transcend ego, find inner peace, and connect with a higher purpose, leading to a more fulfilling and spiritually enriched life.

In essence, forgiveness is an invaluable gift we give ourselves and others. It's a powerful means of letting go of the past, embracing the present, and forging a more compassionate and harmonious future. By forgiving, we can heal, grow, and build stronger, more resilient relationships and communities.

Forgiveness will never happen in one session of contemplation. Instead, it is a new beginning that needs refreshing every day until it becomes your new way of being. What a freeing journey to embark on. It brings you the joy of life and all that comes with it. It will grab you and make you feel the intensity of beautiful emotions. It is love for yourself, everyone around you, and the world.

CASE STUDY FROM THE GLOBAL MASTERMIND COMMUNITY

At the beginning of the year, members of my Mastermind community come together to work on making resolutions to prepare for success. Activities include creating a memory board and writing a forgiveness letter before making the New Year's vision board. Before setting our future visions, we must let go of any old resentments that tie us to the past. Many women especially enjoy this sequence.

Meryam is a teacher from Marrakesh. She was so dedicated to applying each lesson I shared. She was so diligent with her homework. One exercise in particular changed her life. We start the forgiveness practice by writing a forgiveness letter to ourselves and one to each person we hold a grudge against. Beginning the practice of forgiveness is a thorough and robust process. Many of us don't realize how much resentment we carry with us. Our beliefs about how we have failed and how others have betrayed us take tons of energy to maintain. Once you acknowledge it, you can begin the essential step of forgiveness. I admire how she changed her life, specifically how she transformed her relationship with her mother.

FORGIVENESS WILL SET YOU FREE

Yet, it is the hardest thing you can achieve. The only way to let go is to cut the cord with all the hurt from the past.

Let go of anything holding you back and no longer serving you. By "serving you," I mean whether it helps you move forward or not. If you feel it's weighing you down and leaving you emotionally scattered, that's a sign. It's the feeling you get when you try to avoid thinking about it.

If you don't forgive, you will keep holding on to the rage, disappointment, and frustrations from the past. But forgiveness is the hardest thing you can achieve—it is the only way to free yourself and feel enlightened.

Forgiving is the start if you want to elevate your life and move to another sphere of possibilities.

ACTIVITY FOR CODE 2

T his activity challenges you to face where you need to forgive yourself and others to clear the energy so you can move on.

1. Where do you need to forgive yourself?

What are the things you want to forgive yourself for? (Make a list of your perceived most significant errors and failings)

———————————————————————————
———————————————————————————
———————————————————————————
———————————————————————————

Let's forgive ourselves some more. What other things, maybe not colossal life mistakes, but more minor things, you can name clearly?

2. Who else do you need to forgive?

Who do you carry rage against? Make a list. Can you forgive them?

———————————————————————————
———————————————————————————
———————————————————————————

Forgiveness Letters

On a separate paper, write your forgiveness letters. Write until you have nothing else to add.

Directions:

After you complete your forgiveness letter(s), burn or tear them up to release the trapped energy.

Is there another one you need to write? Even though it's hard, try again because now you know how much it will free you.

I commit to forgiving myself.

I plan time to forgive myself actively

I have written my forgiveness letter

EMOTIONS

I would have never thought I could talk about love in meetings and business settings, let alone write about it, yet I found myself doing exactly that. I had never been melodramatic about emotions and sentiments or expressive about my feelings. I grew up very conservative and shy around expressive feelings and could not get myself to hear them, let alone talk about them.

I would have never used "LOVE" to discuss leadership or business strategy in the past. Hearing it in a business setting would make me blush and hide under the table, simply because it was not the correct space for it, and we did not grow up comfortable around it.

My little girl, Zahraty, as I love to call her—meaning "my flower" in Arabic—and the fourth child in the family became the spokesperson for love in the house, loving everyone and speaking it out since she started her first few words.

Zahraty introduced the language of love in the house. Since she could barely speak, she walked everywhere saying, "I love you." It felt pleasing and very soothing to everyone. The more I deepened my work, the more I understood that our mission and everything we do is to spread love and care for humanity.

Many might feel that there is no room for love in banking or anywhere else in the corporate space. I see it differently. Love for humanity brought me to my first mission of development, sustainability, and a world free of poverty at the World Bank.

In the summer of 2023, I was back at the same place where I used to grab hot chocolate every afternoon while working there. I use that same attitude in everything I do—I didn't use the word "love" for it, but I know this is what it is. When love becomes lacking, it is a sign to return to the fundamentals.

The fact that I started my career at a Developmental Institution and have spent years learning, growing, and contributing has shaped me. I learned to give my best in everything I do, to show love and dedication to the overall mission development, and to own every part of it, as it has become my driving force daily.

CODE 3
THE POWER OF LOVE

When you are at rock bottom, you feel loveless and unloveable. But it is precisely at this moment that you need love the most: when you think you are not worthy of it.

In addition, when you don't know you are worthy of love, you can't offer it to your family, work, or the world.

When we are young and we get hurt, we cry, and someone comforts us and tells us it will all be okay. When we become adults, people tell us to suck it up, take responsibility, and that no one will come to our rescue. And yet, everyone has an opinion. You will feel bombarded by points of view, the exclamation "it's your fault" kind of dialogue, and the hardest one was from my own family: "I am so surprised how you turned out to be."

You will do everything to avoid those feelings. You can hang on to science and logic, but if you don't honor emotions, they will haunt you forever.

So, let's find out what is missing in the equation here. That will be emotional intelligence.

EMOTIONAL INTELLIGENCE

Emotional Intelligence (EI) is the ability to manage one's own emotions and understand the feelings of others. It has five key elements: self-awareness, self-regulation, motivation, empathy, and social skills.

One of the leading specialists of emotional intelligence defines* it as the ability to understand, use and manage one's emotions to reduce stress and develop the skills to connect, communicate and understand others. Emotional intelligence builds solid relationships and connections. It involves four key attributes: self-management, self-awareness, social awareness, and relationship management.

The self-management is about mastering your emotions to avoid impulsive behavior and adapt to all circumstances. It helps you process difficult news without losing control, keeping your presence and a logical mind. Self-awareness is about recognizing and honoring them to let them pass. The more you master your emotional intelligence, the more you grow full of empathy and love, enhancing your social awareness and understanding of a group's dynamic. Finally, it is about managing the relationships with yourself and everyone around you.

Emotional intelligence gives you the skills to embrace the duality of life—the tickling and happy emotions, the difficult ones, and being sad and glad simultaneously. The more you can bear and breathe through all the feelings, the more you can prepare to feel and master them.

You need to be aware of a duality in life and integrate it into everything you do. Many people fear passion and doing something they love. They prefer to settle for average, at times mediocre, because everything is average, and there is nothing to worry about when you lose it. In addition, the hurt won't be so profoundly intense.

Passionate relationships and choices are incredibly intense, igniting love and beauty while awakening profound feelings. However, they can also be frightening. When they end, the pain can feel deep and unbearable. This fear often leads people to avoid hurt, preventing them from embracing their passion. Instead, return to love and recognize the growth and wisdom that emerge when things don't go as you hoped.

---

* https://www.helpguide.org/articles/mental-health/emotional-intelligence-eq.htm

Don't be afraid of your feelings. Embrace all of them; honor each emotion and allow them to pass through you.

Emotions will pass when you let them go. You must stay true to yourself without pretending or hiding your feelings. It does not reduce anything about you. It makes you more alive and present. The most powerful lesson about this Code is to simultaneously enhance your ability to feel sad and happy.

ANCHOR YOUR EMOTIONS IN LOVE

When emotions are high, our intelligence is low. When too many emotions take over, it is hard to remember logic and reasoning. Emotions need to be honored for what they are, left to flow in and out easily: there are no constraints and no need to numb them.

With these three first codes, you can breathe through feelings and anchor them back to love and the basics of our humanity. Sometimes, life can be so scary and intense that you wonder how to manage yourself.

Your inner power matches your emotional intelligence. Inner power is essential, and it is crucial to believe in yourself first, then lead yourself and be in charge of what is happening in your life.

When you fall in love with someone at first sight, it awakens something so powerful inside you that you don't know where it came from and how it all happens. It feels like fireworks and makes you fall in love with how you feel around them. Suddenly, there is a sense of freedom with music playing like a Broadway show. You want to dance and fly. You want to have those feel-good moments last forever. That's oxytocin, a hormone you produce that makes you see "la vie en rose" (see life through pink lenses). This type of oxytocin doesn't last more than a few months when it comes from the outside. But you could produce it daily by romanticizing and loving every part of you. After the awakening, this will be the beginning of your emotional mastery.

Emotions make us feel alive. We crave them, look for them, and love that feeling of losing ourselves in them. They make us feel present and excited, entertaining the force of passion from the inside. Emotions make us dream and bring meaning to our lives.

We want to attract more of these experiences because they spice up our lives and create lasting memories. At the same time, we must acknowledge life's duality when things take a turn. Honoring all types of emotions reflects your inner power. When it rains, and the sky is gray, a rainbow appears as soon as the sun shines. We must embrace the rainbow frequency to truly understand duality—the good and the bad, the hard and the soft, the easy and the difficult—existing all at once.

Reconnect with Emotional Comfort

When you go through hard times and challenging experiences, you want to be careful about who you surround yourself with. If you talk too much about the problems you are going through. All you get is their point of view, their take, their way of feeling useful, and that they care. It will feel like a repeated lullaby to an already desperate self. It will become unbearable. You don't want to be in the victim's seat when you strive for leadership. A place you should never let yourself entertain, not even as an option.

Take time to retrieve what is inside you–it is called introspection. Turn off your phone's ringer if it helps you quiet down. You may even want to disconnect from the world. Reconnect with nature instead and find peace in meditation.

Silence will give you space to calm down and put things into perspective.

Particularly if you have a scientific mind, you need to give something logical for the brain to back the spiritual and energetic side because a scientific mind will always look for something to chew on. We spend our time looking for why–when everything is going so smoothly on a career path, storms need to happen.

Thus, I was busy studying how women became successful leaders and multi-millionaires. I went back through time from the beginning when the first women were allowed to go to university, going through

Nobel prize winners into CEOs and billion-dollar unicorn holders. I wanted proof that you can live again, even after a setback. And get evidence that you can recreate yourself and be reborn from your ashes–like a phoenix. I was looking for a clue. It was not only possible but somehow a blessing in disguise. They recreated themselves. They rose bigger than ever before. Women were amazing. So many role models made it through—I was impressed and relieved. I did my therapy by looking at history. I found abundant evidence that people achieved it, making it possible for others. I was looking for a secret I could apply to my life.

Love every story that inspires you or reflects the life you aspire to live. Appreciate people for their sacrifices to create a better life for themselves and others. Honor them for believing in themselves and finding courage in places where it often seems impossible. Cherish their bravery in leadership.

In the energetic language, this is how you calibrate to role models–successful women in this case–by sending them love. You will start feeling it growing inside of you.

Applying this in your life will have an incredible impact beyond your imagination. You will start forgiving yourself as you find evidence of women who recreated themselves to become even more successful and knowledgeable.

It is all about love!

COURAGE COMES FROM UNCONDITIONAL LOVE

The moment you connect with the basic understanding of the power of love, you start building more courage and letting hope grow in you. We need hope to fuel our lives because hope triggers the courage to do so. *Where do you get that courage from?*

During springtime this year, my 6-year-old spent three months singing "Heal the World" by Michael Jackson as part of her class performance. She felt aligned with the big mission of giving hope to every child and spreading peace and love around the globe. This is an example of the magical frequency of us and togetherness. We heal when we love. We heal when we share the love without expecting anything in return. We heal when we are part of one united cause. So, let's make everything about love!

We all need healing from past trauma, from circumstances and events that can take you by surprise. It makes you lose the meaning of who you are and might push you to start hating yourself. A lot of forgiveness and a repetitive mantra that "everything is going to be okay" is the best recipe for feeling okay.

To me, the most potent recipe of all was the unconditional love of my children. I didn't need to ask, but looking into the eyes of my three daughters one day after a tumultuous meeting, I found love. I saw pure love through their shiny little eyes looking at me. I heard their inner voices: "We will love you no matter what."

Every leader needs a voice to comfort them and create a safety net. This book is about leadership and letting the legend in you rise to take you to the highest level of leadership in your life and your role. That leader needs courage. Courage comes from the unconditional love around you, which is why you want to nurture the relationships around you so that you can find love when you need it most. It is okay to let others see your vulnerability.

Humans strive to be loved and appreciated for who they are and what they do. Love is the essence of our being. When we feel love, empathy, and care for ourselves, we have more to give to the rest of the world. Oprah Winfrey once said that when loving oneself, even if others consider it "full of yourself," let yourself be that way. You want to fill your cup with so much love that it runs over. Because if you don't have it for yourself, you will never have anything to give to anyone.

Finally, leaders need the courage to face doubt and carry on. For that, they require unconditional love from others. Therefore, nurturing a close circle of loved ones, friends, or family is essential—and that could be just one person. We are social animals, and it is hard to thrive in isolation, even though everything starts from within.

LOVE YOURSELF AND SPREAD IT OUT

It all starts from within, so forgiveness is the first step. By forgiving yourself, you reconnect with your humanity and the first feeling of purity and love. You start appreciating and understanding who you are. When you do so, you make space to fill your heart with love. As a result, that love will fill your cup, making you radiate so much of it.

You attract to yourself the energy you are aligning with. When you hate yourself, you will magnetize people who treat you wrong and dismiss you with no respect or consideration. Look around. Who are you surrounding yourself with?

If you lack respect and love, it is time to change your inner attitude and reshape your relationship with yourself. How you relate to yourself will define how others connect and relate to you.

Your relationship with yourself is the most important one. You want to cherish you, love you, respect you, and value yourself. You might feel and tell yourself things like: "When I have money, I will. "When I get promoted, I will." Or "When I have my new house, a husband, a child..." The list can be very long and complicated.

It is so simple when we understand it. You attract what you believe to be true love. And your ability to attract love is tightly linked to how much you feel worthy of it. It becomes possible once you have forgiven yourself.

YOU START FIRST; THE REST FOLLOWS

You love yourself first, and everything else will follow. It is a reprogramming.

When you spend so many years dismissing and self-sabotaging yourself, it becomes a tough habit to change. You need to reprogram your subconscious mind. It is as simple as looking at yourself and appreciating who you see.

Promise to strengthen, empower, and become proud of yourself one day. Doing so allows you to step into possibilities, where anything becomes achievable when you believe. So, how can you dismiss the main character of your own life and journey? It's impossible.

You cultivate self-love by feeling deep gratitude for your past self, expressing gratitude in the present, and actively forgiving yourself for perceived mistakes from the past.

Let this be an invitation to love yourself genuinely. Reconnect with the purity of your heart and recognize its innocence. Find peace with your past and forgive yourself for not knowing better. Ignorance may have hindered many dreams and possibilities, but self-development encourages you to ask the right questions and reflect on your life. This process strengthens your inner resilience and helps you make sense of your experiences. Ultimately, your work will become about spreading love for yourself and those around you.

To reprogram yourself effectively, you must consistently affirm that you attract only love and respect into your life.

You need to be open to positive changes to reinforce your subconscious mind. I began interpreting every sign that resonated with me. I felt immense emotion when reading messages from my clients, experiencing the genuine love from the women I had the privilege of meeting, knowing, and helping to grow their businesses and relationships. This connection brought me the most significant rewards.

When I saw women falling in love with their lives again inside our programs, I knew I had a mission. And as days and months unfolded, my whole story made more and more sense. My calling is clear: I want to be a catalyst for change at a more elevated level. And I cannot see a level higher than the one of love, joy, and peace of mind.

The moment you get the spur, you will be open to more magic, and more love will pour every day into your life, enhancing the feeling of being grateful and fulfilled with all of it. You need to master how to manufacture self-love on your own. It starts with the first code of connecting with deep gratitude for yourself from the past and for the present moment. Only then will you be ready for the second code, forgiving yourself for all the perceived errors in the past. Love will replace everything else, and this is what you want more in your life because the frequency of love is the frequency of abundance and prosperity.

Integrating Love Into All Settings

The most significant corporations stand out not only because of their leadership but also because of their deep connection with their "why." They connect with their clients through the why behind their products and services. Connection means an emotional bond. The more the why is associated with love for others and humanity, the more it grows.

Your core values and deeper mission are the same when you anchor them in love. With this dedication, you can carry out any work you carry as an executive, an entrepreneur, a mentor, a strategist, a consultant, or a professional. Love would transcend to every part of it.

In the same way, the World Bank slogan, "A dream of a world free of poverty," made everyone at the World Bank feel that what they do is way beyond a paycheck; it has an impact that is more significant than their own. It creates a genuine connection and love for the mission. **When you love your work, it is called passion; when you don't, it's called stress.**

Choose a mission that mirrors the true love you have inside. My mission today connects with my passion to see women succeed and create wealth for themselves and their families. I built on top of my mission at the World Bank. The more we create wealth, the more we provide. We will be able to fight poverty by creating prosperity.

The same goes for any corporate meeting with a high-level executive of multinationals or big companies. Success, growth, and development are about loving the overarching mission, the daily work, and caring for all the employees. If one is lacking in the equation, there will be no strategy that would replace it. Everything starts with love, grows with love, and stands out with love.

Ultimately, corporations are not about the people who work for them. And people need love for their work to create a true passion. They also need to be appreciated to fuel their productivity and creativity. When you let the loving feeling overwhelm you at work without blockage, shame, or a cold attitude, you open the gate for emotional flow. The feminine energy brings this into a masculine paradigm world. It breathes the force of life into every professional move, as tackled in the following Code.

CASE STUDY FROM THE GLOBAL MASTERMIND COMMUNITY

When you go through trauma, like when Alexa lost her partner a few days before getting married while being in our program, she received so much love and compassion from all the women inside the Mastermind. We held space for her so that she could feel welcomed and understood in the sad moments she was going through. Moments like this are when you need to strengthen your understanding of duality and reconnect with the miracle of being alive as much as possible. No one could ever understand the trauma a person is going through, like Alexa–but we can hold the space for her inside a container that makes her feel safe and loved. That feeling of belonging without needing to force yourself into doing anything is powerful. The healing and the cycle of grief will take the time it needs, and all we want to do is honor it and listen to ourselves. Alexa felt held and is getting her strength back to lead herself through all the responsibilities she inherited.

PROCESSING FEELINGS

Our emotional intelligence allows us to process our feelings. We should not seek validation or justification for our feelings from the mind. Instead, we should allow them to flow through us smoothly and effortlessly. If we get into the mind to validate all the feelings, we transform them and become controlled by them. Thus, sadness would turn into rage instead of letting it pass and waiting for the law of rhythm to return happiness. This is how healing becomes effective and makes sense when it helps understand the depth of your emotions.

There is a magnetism when you are in tune with your feelings and emotions. So, if you want to bring that magnetism into your life to elevate your leadership style and reach high professional success, you must start with the foundation. And that is the paradigm. It is the inner software or programming inside our subconscious mind. And it is all about emotions.

FINDING PURE LOVE WITHIN

It is all about finding the source of love inside you and letting it compound. It becomes the starting point to project more love in the future and all the prosperity that aligns with it. We often connect love to pleasing and being validated through it. In this case, love is seen more like a trade, and with time, it becomes a self-fulfilling prophecy inside our subconscious mind.

It feels empty and hollow when you stop pleasing everyone when everything is based on calculated interests. When love is connected to pleasing, the moment you decide that you no longer want to be the pleaser, you will find yourself loveless if you haven't created your source of love from within.

Pleasing cannot be sustained forever, while love is infinite. Love should be unconditional. Love is passion, purpose, and a sense of meaning. With that lens, we can bring love to all we do, both in life and work, even in the most extensive corporate settings.

Focus on what excites you and what you are passionate about. Feel the sensation of joy, knowing that you are a channel of the divine. You are indeed an embodiment of love.

ACTIVITY FOR CODE 3

Tap into and enhance your emotional intelligence around love.

List three people you admire and look up to.

    1.

    2.

    3.

Using the people listed above: Relate to them with love for what they do and who they are. Articulate three things you love about each that you want to align yourself with.

    1.

_____

_____

_____

_____

    2.

_____

_____

_____

_____

3.

_____

_____

_____

_____

We align with the feeling of love and admiration, and not jealousy and envy. Send vibes of love and affection.

Take this to the next level: Call or write to each of these people to express your love and admiration.

LINEAGE

A Homage to my grandmother Amna.

My Grandmother Amna played a central role in my upbringing. I was in total admiration of her beauty and resilience.

Amna was illiterate yet a renowned designer of elegant modern dresses for the ladies in Sfax, Tunisia. She was confident, a mother of 6, an exquisite cook, and a modern woman. She had extended so much love and trust in me, her granddaughter—I always felt overwhelmed by her caring.

My Grandmother raised my beautiful Mum with all the confidence, resilience, and grace she represented. The deepening of my understanding of the lineage reconnected me with my roots and the force of life I carry from my ancestors. I am who I am today because of my Mum and my Grandmother. They had me within themselves pre-conception, and I take them with me today wherever I go and in everything I do, every touch, every feeling—they all live in me.

My sisters and I were incredibly blessed to be surrounded by remarkable role models. My mom taught us to celebrate being women, command respect, believe in ourselves, and use our intelligence. She showed us how to navigate male-dominated environments confidently and appreciate the beauty around us, attracting it with ease and flow. She also encouraged us to desire for others what we want for ourselves.

I have a profound appreciation for this heritage, which embodies a love for the beauty of life, a commitment to excellence, and a first-class attitude. It reflects a love for caring and helping and a passion for giving and serving humanity.

This connection fuels my admiration for every woman who honors her lineage, represents her heritage, and leaves behind a meaningful legacy.

Celebrate your best expression of being and share it as an inspiring story.

For every woman reading this code: You are every woman!

You are a beautiful woman and a mother, a legacy for all your lineage, and a great leader.

And if you are a man reading this, it gives you a sense of a deeper understanding of feminine energy and women's emotional behavior.

CODE 4
THE FORCE OF LIFE

B y now, you are starting to believe more and more in the incredible human being you are, the love you carry inside, and the wisdom you can draw from your story and the past. Code 4 is a beautiful piece of the puzzle to embrace feminine energies, complete your belief in yourself and the universe's potentialities, and dive into the world of energetics.

WHY DO WE TALK ABOUT ENERGETICS?

This whole code is about connecting and aligning with your emotional strength. This is about feeling the roots of the miracle of creation. Each woman can become in tune with how her body can carry a new life inside and be part of that miracle.

This code can be one of the most potent transmissions that connect us with the essence of life and the depth of our inner power. It is a contemplation moment for you to reconnect with the spirit of life. It is also the embodiment of feminine energy.

There is power in connecting with your spiritual perfection and using it to plug into the light within and infinite intelligence. This is more about *being and feeling* than taking *action and doing*. Depending on situations and circumstances, we embody several archetypes, and the one you want to start by mastering is the one connected with the power within. It is about being and grounding at every moment.

Bringing Energetics Into Your Identities

To lead yourself, you need to master the different characteristics inside of you. When you know these personas, how they behave, and how to unlock the enigma, they become your allies. You can channel them into your business.

The three archetypes that matter the most are:

1. **The warrior** and the active side of you who uses masculine energy to accomplish and do things,
2. **The divine** or the goddess or the sovereign in you that connects you with being who you are,
3. **The boss** is the leader and the master of vision and strategy. This is a hybrid of both the masculine and the feminine energy.

Being aware of the different identities makes you appreciate every step you take. It is also the start of understanding what emotions activate in you through your journey and how to react to them.

You don't feel fulfilled because of all your achievements, what you have created, or the projects you have completed. Fulfillment comes from finding meaning in what you do. It is also about being connected with the feelings you have when you achieve your work and embark on anything you do.

When meaning is lost, you will feel that you are always running after your objectives. As soon as you reach one, another objective shows up. The run never stops; it will feel like a never-ending hamster wheel or running on a treadmill without going anywhere.

That feeling is exacerbated by the lack of time to do it all. You become overwhelmed by the tasks and responsibilities and stressed about time and deadlines.

An essential step to elevating the leader in you is to be aware of the different identities that you have inside you. You can use each of the identities to strengthen yourself and to understand the uniqueness you are made of. These identities come with different types of energetics and styles. When you learn to embody each one, you will suddenly rise to reach the success you aspire to achieve.

1. THE IDENTITY OF THE WARRIOR, THE ACTIVE DOER IN YOU

This identity is about doing. It embodies your capacity to take on any project and do it well and on time. When the warrior identity is activated, you know you can take on mountains and do them so well that you can even surprise yourself.

You write the to-do list and go through every item individually. You know how to make sure that each one is executed correctly. This way, you get ready again to start the next one on that to-do list. However, it ends up feeling like running after a never-ending to-do list.

This identity finds roots in the masculine paradigm we grow up with. Going to school is all about doing the homework, learning the lessons, passing the exams, and having good grades. These good grades are so important so that you can get into the best universities and prepare for that interview for the best job. It doesn't even stop there. It continues as you go on the track to more responsibilities, becoming a manager, and later having a cozy retirement.

The key lies in continuous action. This constant doing often drives us to seek even more to accomplish. Active warriors focus solely on action, working hard and filling their days with tasks. However, this identity can lead to feeling overwhelmed and burned out, especially when we add the nagging sense that we are never doing enough.

2. *The identity of the divine, the goddess in you*

This identity was new to me at the beginning of my self-development journey. I didn't know how it could help us change our lives when we integrated it. When I started integrating its understanding and meaning three years ago, it echoed my most profound knowledge of fulfillment. This identity is the force of life. It is the power inside you; it is your connection with the universe, mother nature, infinite intelligence ... the divine.

This identity is the one that helps you reconnect with who you are and celebrate every step with gratitude for what you have. This is about feelings. You own the divine in you and honor the goddess for female leaders. It is about feeling good, aligned, and connected with your inner drive, values, and mission. It takes a moment to anchor the why behind your work and services. It helps bring meaning to everything you do and enables you to enjoy every step of your journey. Success is not about doing different things. It is about how you feel when you do what you do. Make it a celebration and an honoring of the incredible soul you have inside you as you do your work!

3. *The identity of the boss and the great leader*

This identity is the most powerful, combining the feminine energy, which connects with the divine in you, with the masculine paradigm of the warrior and the doer. This identity is about finding harmony while defining your best-fit strategy. The strategist is the boss in you—the one who contemplates every move, anchors every success, and gets ready for growth and evolution.

This identity comes from the wisdom in you and the leader that helps you articulate your action plan and magnetize all the opportunities for you. All this while mastering your emotional intelligence and understanding the energetics behind each identity.

IGNITING THE FORCE OF LIFE

The force of life lives in you. You have it inside. There is a voice within us and a connection that resonates from within. It is not about doing something or taking action but about feeling it and being.

You must return to your heart and what you feel to heal and elevate yourself. Returning to feelings is the only way to recover from within and strengthen yourself. This is why the Force of Life Code comes after forgiveness and love. Without forgiveness, you cannot break free; every thought will be about punishment, anger, and revenge. The Divine is about forgiveness and love. That liberating feeling occurs in the energy of emotions.

Embarking on the emotional voyage within is the portal to the most remarkable comeback of your life. It will empower you from within with infinite desire, focus, and power and elevate you to the next level. This is how to reignite your soul and magnetize new opportunities and significant results.

You must understand that the Divine and the higher force live in you. She is the one who saved you from everything, who helped you survive through all the events and circumstances, and who is making you whole and fulfilled. As women, we need to reconnect with the incredible power we have in our bodies and how we can tap into it to radiate like a spark of light.

Your actions do not define the divine, the force of life. Instead, it lies in your ability to access this force through a state of being and to see how much meaning you can create in your life. Therefore, when you experience something painful, the issue is not the hurt itself but the meaning you assign to it. The force of life is not about what you need to do or what you can accomplish; it's about how you connect with yourself and explore what lies within you. This connection helps you transcend the circumstances surrounding you.

AWAKEN THE SPIRIT OF LIFE

Music has been my actual therapy throughout my journey. Various songs came to mind during various chapters of my life and felt in harmony. I found peace and elevation in The Lion King's music, which celebrates the Spirit that lives in us because the source of life is within.

The Lion King's performance in the song "He Lives in You" was about igniting the source of life from within and all the strength that comes with it. There is infinite light inside of us if we can tap into it and where we see the fine line between science, logic, and spirituality. Last summer, I spent a week with my family in Disney World—an entire week of Marvel, princesses, parks, and sparks. Every day with my children, I celebrated the beauty of life, the joy of living, and just being together in an enchanting setup. I watched the Broadway musical Lion King repeatedly, and each time the old and wise person told Simba the young lion, "He lives in you," I felt my tears rolling down my cheeks. I needed that spirit to remind me where the power and feeling safe find its root. It is all inside. I keep it in my heart:

> "The spirit of life ...calling
> And a voice, with the fear of a child
> Answers...
>
> Wait, there is no mountain too great
> Hear the words and have faith...
> Have faith
>
> He lives in you
> He lives in me
>
> He watches over
> Everything we see
> Into the water, into the truth
> In your reflection, He lives in you."

These words resonated so much with me. I connect with each one of them. I feel each one of them. It became my daily little moment of elevation and musical meditation.

It was growing more every day. I felt more robust, and I moved to the beat. I knew how real this was. There is light in you, me, and all of us

—it's time for you to tap into it and let it guide you. Create a space of acknowledgment, love, and forgiveness—the light will take over and radiate to magnetize more of it back to you.

FLOW OF FEMININE ENERGY

There is incredible power in our body and how we are connected with it. There are things you cannot explain in words but can ignite, feel, and trust their existence. This is feminine energy—the very energy that precedes your being. It is essential to understand here that both genders carry feminine energy.

Feminine energy represents the purity of the more prominent force within you. The divinity within is the identity of the Sovereign or the one that makes you who you are and feels all the vibes around you. This code is the most potent transmission because of the understanding of the power of BEING. You don't need to do anything; you deserve it all because of your identity. It is about the source within, the one that guides us and feeds us with all the energy, motivation, and inspiration within.

This is how to make your life more meaningful: squeeze every drop out of your surroundings and extract its essence to create your story and become a beautiful reference.

It ignites all the senses and makes you appreciate the meaning of every little thing we once could have been taken for granted. This is when you sit by the water watching the sunset or at the full moon and feel nature wrapping every inch of your being. It awakens your awareness about everything around you. You feel alive, emotional, and on top of your game.

The more you know and experience your feelings, the more you feel alive. Emotions as they come - happy and sad—you connect to the beauty of each one of them in their context and timing. This code is for you to tap into the frequency that makes you feel alive and understand the infinite potential you have within. Because the Divine, mother nature, the endless intelligence—as you like to see it, is all that brings you home into who you indeed are, into the very creation of your being.

This is you touching the force inside. You don't need to do anything; you just need to BE.

In other words, we can capture all the meaning of our lives. We want to create space for it to exist and grow. Feminine energy is a connection with the force of creation–which we all have inside us. In particular, for women, all that energy is concentrated in the womb, and the incredible miracle of creation starts inside it.

The identity of the divine, the goddess, or the sovereign embodies a landscape of emotion. When ready to heal, you embrace that identity, recognizing that your feelings shape you. This recognition allows you to recover when the time is right or to let the emotional process unfold at its own pace.

The identity of the divine will lift you as it brings you peace and well-being, not holding on to rage and resentment, and, more importantly, loving you deeply. Finally, feminine energy is the creation energy that comes from the source within. It is who you are and not what you do. I call it sacral energy because it carries multiple codes and keys within this code itself. It spreads indefinitely through the web of time and space.

POWER FINDS ROOT IN YOUR LINEAGE

Every human being fits into a long and perfectly defined lineage. We are a gateway from the past to the future. We carry all the heritage from years and years before, encompassed with traditions, culture, stories, emotions, and the history of time. And we craft the very legacy we will leave behind for future generations.

You were carried in your mother's womb during the whole nine months of gestation. But before that, the ovule, the egg of your creation, lived in your mother's body all the years before you were born. Even earlier than that, as your mother was going through the gestational period in your grandmother's womb, you were there too, a microscopic egg that existed before your mum and before you. We live inside our ancestors' bodies for years before we open our eyes and make the first scream. They shape us, and they leave a mark on our very DNA. We carry all the emotions we lived inside our mother's and grandmother's bodies. Women fascinate me and connect so much with my empowerment and leadership work.

When we plant a seed of love and peace inside a woman, it is not just for her; it is for all the generations that come after her. It becomes integrated into the lineage of her very existence.

We are here to carry a bigger vision. It must start from the inside if we want to change and positively impact the world. The moment I understood and contemplated this eye-opening reality, something shifted in me forever.

I was able to find innocence in the mistreatment I might have felt throughout my life from anyone around me, from a mother who did not understand me when I needed her most. From my siblings and the little but hurtful quarrels, we keep inside us. We are all so connected, but it confuses us if we don't understand all the emotions of those interactions.

But the winner of all of this is that forgiveness became easier. If you cannot do it for the person, do it for her lineage—the one before and after. A person's behavior or attitude, no matter how bad and hurtful that could be, has nothing to do with the lineage and the right for the next generation to have a peaceful and loving life. For the sake of our children, let's be the change. Bring the change by starting a pure wave of love and peace. There is a force so strong in you that it will radiate and reach out to millions. Everything reverberates and gets compounded astonishingly. We often get so busy and excited about what's coming next that we miss this understanding.

We have lost so much of that meaning from our positioning in our lineage. And in that spree, we lost much about what we have inside us. That very meaning does not come from achievements. It comes from our ability to create what we have in our line as you build your legacy.

This is a reclamation to honor women for their being, for what they carry in their body, and for what she was once part of. We are a tiny piece of the giant puzzle of life.

Because we are a portal of the divine and the more prominent force, we embody the sacred feminine energy when we understand and feel the beauty of womanhood. This is when we can navigate through the real emotions and impose them on top of our three-dimensional reality of the material world. Call it intuition, feelings, or the sixth sense. It is a reclamation of the effortlessness of our creation and an honoring of who we are within our lineage and the legacy we create.

We want to bring meaning to our existence, creation, and identity. If not, our legacy gets lost repetitively and mechanically of being.

Become the Best Version of You

We are born powerful and have all the potential. We are born with our source of life and have kept it inside of us. It is a portal of creation and manifestation. Awareness of its existence opens a crack of light—so small we often dismiss it. But it grows, becoming a beacon impossible to miss when we know it.

There is a reason why we are born when we are. Nothing happens haphazardly. Everything is interconnected and synchronized. The more you believe in it, the more you will see proof of it unfolding in front of your eyes. Your existence is structured around your footprint, astrological identity, and emotional pattern. Our role is to make our lives the best representation of our being.

You need to embody this today: using feminine energy to navigate through the labyrinth of life while aligning with the energetics of the universe and infinite potential. This creates miracles and magnetizes beauty, love, money, prosperity, and incredible success.

Thus, your job should be to become the best version of yourself, align with evolution, seek personal growth and wisdom, and give your best in everything you offer and work.

We want to turn our existence into the best expression of who we are by reflecting all these universal realities, the seen and the unseen.

Case Study from the Global Mastermind Community

This part about the lineage shows why this code applies to women and their connection with their mothers and grandmothers. This part helps women start the healing of mother's wounds–and there is unanimity inside our women-only Mastermind regarding how essential it is to reconnect with the roots. Yasmine, a mother of two adolescents, was not able to reconnect with her mother without holding on to the rage about how controlling she was when she was young and still is. The understanding of the lineage and the work of letting go of all the negativity by reconnecting with the force of life is so liberating. Thus, through intentional reprogramming of the subconscious mind and healing meditations, Yasmine started redefining her relationship with herself and her mother. This healing helped her become a better mother to her children.

ACTIVITY FOR CODE 4

L ook at yourself in the mirror.

Look at yourself and smile.

There is only one of you. So unique. There will never be anyone exactly like you!

Today, you are the youngest you will ever be.

Celebrate today and feel happy.

Boost your energy and bring fun into your life.

It is all in your hands.

The force of life is within you

To take charge of your mind

And overwhelm yourself with happiness.

Be kind to yourself and fill your heart with love.

Kindness starts with yourself.

Do something nice for yourself.

Let go of the bitterness about things from the past
   And embrace today.

RESILIENCE

I call myself a strategist now. I can fully own it now, after 25 years of focused experience articulating all sorts of strategies. At the international level, I spent almost a decade at the World Bank setting up a country-wide, sectoral, and regional strategy. We have studied every side and level of environmental, water, economic, and country strategies.

Going back to a few years earlier, I knew that the decision-making sphere was where everything happened. I was fascinated by those closed meetings where things got strategized and outlined. I was intrigued and drawn to them—all the excitement from decision theory, decision-making, operations research, intelligence, and game theory. My professor, Peter Rogers, was a pro on game theory, researching and discussing it at length. I was his teaching assistant, so I needed to be on top of the whole concept. We attended incredible meetings that brought me chills and excitement in multi-national institutions, the Pentagon, and government offices. I lived through my own "James Bond" movie. I knew everything mattered and that the skills needed to connect the dots would appear vividly in front of my eyes the more I studied and worked on different strategies.

After many years of elaborating, structuring, outlining, and defining strategies for the public sector and corporations, I know that any strategy works as long as it is coherent with the objectives and context. The challenge is defining the proper context and fundamentals to create an unshakable inner drive and a noble mission. At that moment, the strategy will help you achieve the impossible. We reverse engineer from any objective. The beauty of the structuring and the logic that comes with it would outshine any challenges. Then comes the focus and the discipline.

Now, let's dive into how to master the game behind defining the right strategy and your capacity to engineer the best one for your life and your business.

PART TWO
ACT

Be present
Be disciplined
Be excellent in everything you do
Prepare your boldest self for your most significant challenges

Part 2 prepares you to take action by unlocking four codes about planning and discipline and how to set up the best brand for yourself and stand out in your uniqueness as a legend.

CODE 5 – ENGINEER YOUR BEST STRATEGY
CODE 6 – DISCIPLINE YOURSELF
CODE 7-- MAKE EXCELLENCE YOUR BRAND
CODE 8—CREATE THE LEGEND

These codes will help you to:

Think strategically
Reverse engineer the best strategy
Translated into an easy-to-carry-out action plan

Get started in making it your reality.

Hold the emotional void with every strength of your being
    And embrace the Duality of life and hold on to it

Tap into your creativity and let the Legend in you shine.

This is your life, so make it a masterpiece!

Code 5
Engineer Your Best Strategy

L et's do some strategic planning together here. Starting with decision theory and then moving to real-life applications.

Game Theory in Business, Life & Beyond

Mathematics is part of our daily lives. Surprisingly enough, we use mathematics in everything we do, from setting up our monthly budget, grocery shopping, our way of thinking, inner logic, organization of our thoughts, solving complex problems, and daily management of our businesses and companies. Game Theory is the winner. It explains the strategic interactions between agents or *players* in any real-life situation: the relationship between colleagues, family members, friends, and people in general.

Discovered in 1920, Game Theory became a base tool for microeconomics and the modeling of zero-sum games in 1944. More research and 11 Nobel prizes put the theory above economic thinking. It is applied to social science, political science, international relations, biology, business, and organizations. In addition, Game Theory explains frequently seen behaviors in human relations. Notably, the 1950 prisoner dilemma is the most popular as it simplifies understanding treason in business and our relationships.

WHAT IS THE PRISONER DILEMMA?

It illustrates a situation where two players find an interest in cooperating. However, because of a lack of communication, each one would choose to betray the other when the game is played only once. In real life, we get only one shot in an acute situation where decisions can be definitive. The question is, why? Well, if one of the players betrays the other, the cooperator is strongly penalized. If both players betray, results will be less favorable than cooperation.

UNDERSTANDING PEOPLE'S BEHAVIOR THROUGH THE PRISONER DILEMMA

The prisoner dilemma mirrors people's behavior around us, whether in business, among friends, or family members. The concept is used in psychology to treat media rumors, tariff strategy, business competition, and many other domains. To better apprehend its relevance, Princeton Professor Albert Tucker gave the example of two partners in crime kept in two separate cells. They were both presented with three options:

1. If only one of them denounces the other, he gets freed, while the other receives the maximum sentence of 10 years;
2. If they both denounce each other, they get a 5-year sentence;
3. If they both refuse to speak, they get a minimal sentence of 6 months for lack of relevant information.

This theory led to several economic games that tested the players' economic rationale and ability to reach a satisfying equilibrium without deteriorating others' situations. In addition to mathematics and economics, the prisoner dilemma is pertinent to psychoanalysts, ecosystem scientists, biologists, and political science specialists. It is also used in some philosophy paradigms and cognitive science.

Prisoner dilemma is applied in any field whenever two or more agents have a common interest in cooperating. Still, one default is an even more critical interest in not doing so, while there is no way to constrain the other to cooperate. For instance, these are two companies in the same market where one decides to increase the price and inflate the returns. If they both increase the price, they will both lose. In another setting within a team, one member could betray the boss—even wrongly, as he can see himself jumping the ladder hierarchy. Similar situations emerge among associates, partners, and investors in the same fund or structure where there is often a temptation to use similar tactics. In the world of information, the competitiveness in the media business is identical to the prisoner dilemma. Certain media favor information speed before quality, which generates error pooling phenomena.

This prisoner dilemma explains bizarre behavior between a boss and a confused subordinate, a demanding client, a relationship with a toxic person, jealousy, and hostile acquaintances. They all lead to the same point of betrayal, hatred, negative energy, and a spiraling destructive trend and confusion. However, once we understand the logic behind the prisoner dilemma, we can predict betrayal before it even happens. You become a master of your own doing and expectations in your business. This is why any entrepreneur or business owner needs to protect themself by keeping their moves secret and mastering their surroundings—risk analysis and a thorough strategic plan with a clear understanding of their competitor.

We live in a competitive world where treason has become a time and space transcending reality. Treason has found a comfortable seat in all our lives: in our homes, streets, offices, cities, structures, and the most influential organizations. The more fascinating TV shows and series are, the more they reflect this ever-growing phenomenon where cruelty, lies, and fakeness have taken over our societies. Where did the values and manners go? Overblown egos have hijacked humanity, and "I want everything only for myself, and now" by selfishness and greed.

Nevertheless, the planetary meditation dictated by the pandemic and several natural disasters has awakened lost compassion in people's hearts and returned us to the path to goodness, sharing, serenity, love, and abundance. To me, the work we do in the field of self-development is about replanting the seed of love and compassion.

A positive vision of a better world sheds light on more elevated and conscious people and business actors!

A Winning Strategy

It is a game beyond a game!

Leadership is a game that feels so good when you master the rules and navigate through them with soft and light energy. But before playing, you need to set up the correct container, which means the boundaries and the rules that align with who you are because anything can spill if there are cracks in the lining of your container. You will lose yourself before enjoying who you want to be. Setting up a substantial container requires strategic thinking, knowledge, and a mastery of your game, which is strengthened with resilience and perseverance.

It does not matter what happens in your life. It doesn't matter where you are in your life. Everything depends on how you plan your next move. Every moment in time, you have three things in your hands: what you think about, what you feel, and what you do.

None of them will change your life completely, but they can alter its trajectory. To shift from a depressive state to a positive outlook, you need to become the guard of your mind. This was my approach to one of my private clients in investment banking. The pressure on her was so intense it was almost impossible for her to keep a positive outlook. But with the understanding that what we do in the present moment could alter the trajectory of our life, the shift began to be felt little by little in her work environment until she started getting approval for her dedication and ability to stay calm in any situation.

This code is an invitation to think strategically and positively, to take one small action at a time to better yourself and feel good about yourself no matter what. This code relies on your deep belief and understanding that you deserve the best and are ready to accept the best of yourself. Often, we feel overwhelmed by all the difficulties we face and start dismissing ourselves and feeling that we don't deserve anything good. All of this comes from old stories and beliefs we might think have overcome, but they are still there even if we ignore them. It may show up as bad habits about how we treat ourselves.

It is time for us to rewrite our stories. Start by saying that you deserve the best. Stay connected to that firmly, and stay ready to have the best.

When you get to that stage of understanding, you will feel an excitement running through your spine: a feeling of wanting to do everything now and do everything fast to compensate for the time lost. There is no reason to rush anything. What matters in reality is being present and connected with all your feelings at every step, being aware of the present moment and your actions. Anchoring every step by acting on it, the good with more appreciation and the bad by extracting the lessons and the wisdom.

You will only reach high success and fulfillment with a scar. The very definition of success is the ability to stand back up after having fallen.

If this book makes you want to recreate yourself and start new—like a reborn—take this as a sign, and let's do it together.

The good news is that you are not starting from zero. All the experiences and all the knowledge are there to prove otherwise. Therefore, the winning attitude is to choose to focus on the beauty of memories and the wisdom of all the lessons from previous years. Every extracted lesson helps you define the context of that very year.

CASE STUDY FROM THE GLOBAL MASTERMIND COMMUNITY

Samia was not doing the homework diligently or the morning routine. She was attending all the program sessions and just thinking through the homework in her head. So, no changes were happening. She was looking for a job. But, interview after interview, nothing happened. Until one day, on her own, she said–I want to start doing the work as well. Can you help me? We started with creating a board with all her beautiful memories, and she became happier and more confident–she started participating. We continued on all the other sequences of the program. We defined a strategy for her to land her best job. Indeed, in a few weeks, by creating a board with all the beautiful memories that she had, she became happier and more confident. She started participating, and we continued doing what she wanted. We could have started by defining her strategy initially, but it would not have worked. She needed to make the unshakable decision to participate in the program and make the strategy work entirely.

Having a Clear Vision

I want to go back in history and draw one of the most significant leadership lessons from Tarik Ibn Zeyad. He was one of the Greatest Leaders of the 7th and 8th centuries. As a military strategist, he conquered the Iberic Peninsula (Spain and Portugal of today) and started the Muslim Kingdom, which governed until the 11th century.

Tarik Ibn Zeyad's conquest is the biggest lesson of leadership. With a clear vision and by empowering his troops, he led them to victory!

It still applies today to each one of us. Having a clear vision, empowering oneself, and taking action are among the top qualities of successful leadership!

This section highlights Tarik Ibn Zeyad's strategic leadership. It draws from history and today's business world seven leadership qualities to embrace to engineer the best strategy and reach the goals with excellence.

Going back to the conquest of the Iberic Peninsula in the 8th century

One of the history courses that always stuck in my mind was about Tarik Ibn Zeyad and his conquest of the Iberia Peninsula. Tarik Ibn Zeyad gathered around 5000 to 7000 soldiers, largely Berber and Arab troops, trained them and built large ships to cross the sea from Tangier to Spain. When they arrived in Spain, he ordered them to burn the ships, telling his soldiers who did not know how to swim back: **"The sea is behind you, and the enemy is in front of you... Your only way is Victory."**

This is how Tarik Ibn Zeyad brought Muslim civilization to the Peninsula and governed for many years. Gibraltar is named after him. Its Arabic name is the Mountain of Tarik (Jabal Tarek). This is a lesson transcending history about leadership and victory. It reaffirms that one of the best leadership criteria is having a clear vision and empowering your team and followers!

You can apply this to your life by knowing your goal clearly and vividly and cutting every link with the past. In other words, you need to burn bridges so there is no turning back to old life. The only destinations available are "**Success**" and "**Victory**".

SEVEN LEADERSHIP QUALITIES

Drawing from several lessons from history and the modern business world, it needs to include a set of qualities for leadership to be successful. These qualities need to co-exist to create a compelling and empowered leadership style.

1. **A clear vision** distinguishes leaders from managers and transforms them into transformational, inspirational, and responsible individuals.
2. **Courage** is not only the opposite of conformity but also the willingness to take risks with no assurance of success.
3. **Integrity**: All executives and leaders agree that complete honesty in everything you do is essential. This means telling the truth to all people and in all situations.
4. **Humility**: by recognizing the value of others and by empowering followers and people around you.
5. **Strategic planning involves looking ahead and anticipating market trends and opportunities**. Strategy can never be alone; it must be accompanied by all the other characters to work successfully.
6. **Results-focused**: to keep your eyes on what needs to be achieved and to stay laser-focused no matter what.
7. **Excellence**: Leaders seek excellence in their organization, their offer, their work, and their business practices.

The set of qualities and the different ways to adopt the personality of leaders are essential. Nevertheless, it can all be distilled into a single concept: the ability to get results. A leader must set a goal and have the courage and ability to reach it.

Thus, staying focused can happen by always keeping the goal in mind. Instead of focusing on problems or why they cannot reach their goals, leaders spend their energy on finding solutions to overcome obstacles and what could stop them from achieving their pre-set goals.

Drawing from several lessons of historical victories and today's successful leaders, the secret to empowered leadership is having a solid mindset, an unshakable belief in reaching success and a commitment to one's goals. Solutions and possibilities are the overriding themes.

This concept applies to everyone because everyone is a leader in their living and operating space. At home, parents are leaders. In a group of friends, they could take a leadership role when they plan an outing or simply be in charge of ordering a pizza. As entrepreneurs, business owners display leadership in managing their businesses. In an organization, executives show leadership within their team with their expertise and the strategic positioning of their work.

Finally, your leadership footprint depends on your mindset and the impact you want to have.

A clear vision and the courage to reach it will determine your leadership success!

USE THE MEANING OF CONTEXT TO CREATE YOUR VISION

As you grow in maturity and experience, every year and every chapter of your life will unfold with a new context. When you pile them one after the other, they will align with your vision.

I want to share here how it helped me in my own life. I give context to every year, just as if I had given them a clear theme. Last year was the year of gratitude and love. Every journey I embarked on was filled with gratitude and experienced from the angle of sharing love with my family, clients, and the community around me.

After feeling overwhelmed and faced with challenges as an

entrepreneur for several years, I have become intentional about pausing and feeling gratitude for every step. When you do that, you will appreciate how any walk for success needs to have every step grounded in appreciation. You stand on the ground, with one foot planted in gratitude and the next one toward your aspirations and desires. You are moving away from challenges and overcoming difficulties.

This realization is so powerful! It changes your journey. It isn't about running a never-ending race, looking for the next goal and objective. This journey of success is filled with thanksgiving and celebrations for every step, no matter how small. As you deepen your understanding of mindset and energetics and how they intertwine with strategy and planning, you will approach the New Year's resolution and planning differently.

We never start from zero. We accumulate our understanding of life, its wisdom and its lessons year after year in both the professional and personal spheres. Finding a context that will become the year's overriding theme helps you select the lens you will use for everything you do. The context is the theme you choose so that you can build upon the past and get closer to your vision for yourself and throughout your life.

Without a strong context, you don't leave anything to interpretation or confusion. It helps you ask the right questions when faced with a dilemma in your business or any part of your personal life.

Resilience and Introspection

My context moved from a year of "Resilience" in 2020 to "Introspection" in 2021. It was all about understanding the mindset, the old paradigm, and the energetics, in addition to launching my work in self-development as a mentor and executive coach. That's when I created the BAL Method and made the three-step process easy for every woman to:

- Believe in herself and the possibilities by strengthening her mindset and energetics while understanding the science of success.
- Act on her goal by turning it into a strategic plan, clarifying her branding and positioning in the market.

- Lead herself excellently, using her genius, providing excellent value and consistency, which will build trust and credibility.

What I want to add to this process today is its connection to wealth creation and establishing a new money paradigm. Recreating the money story starts with understanding your actual value and how to connect with a frequency beyond money, that of prosperity and currency— paving the way to a new context to embody.

Growth and Evolution

For me, 2023 was a year of growth and evolution, building upon all the previous contexts of resilience, introspection, gratitude, and love. Not that my years before 2020 did not mean anything, but I didn't bring this much intentionality to the power of energetics as I do today.

My focus was more on the objectives and themes of their living and operating space. Some years, I was focused on professional aspects, while others centered on personal matters. The beauty now is realizing, with time and experience, that balance exists in everything. You cannot set one aspect aside to fix another. You will constantly juggle everything and feel unsatisfied forever.

This context of growth and evolution goes beyond business. It applies to relationship building, connections, clients, and global impact. Seeing how it spreads beyond business and my role as a mentor and business strategist by launching different programs and working with incredible women worldwide is stunning. It encompasses being a mother, a wife, a sister, a daughter, a family member, a friend, and a connection. In addition, this context makes the year feel like a lifetime of growth and evolution without putting pressure and stress on tight deadlines. Ground every step in gratitude and gear the next toward growth and evolution.

As I continue writing this book in 2024, it will be a year of creativity for me to face challenges, develop my business, and attract new opportunities. It is also about elegance in everything I do, how I write, respond and carry myself in any situation.

Finally, it is essential to be aware of what you are compounding in your journey of growth and evolution. Is it a perspective of success or anxious thoughts about what comes next?

Defining your context helps you set the right tone; being intentional in every move and genuinely present in everything you do will change your life this year and elevate your leadership!

Diving Into the World of Finance

Multinational and International Financial Institutions have always fascinated me. They handle billions every day. In particular, I was amazed at how they structure everything and manage and dispatch financial instruments to projects implemented worldwide.

Once you have been in the middle of that, it opens your mind to millions of possibilities.

Everything becomes connected and interdependent. We are who we are because of all those transactions. We can become part of them when we rise, believe, and align with all those realities.

We could also hide and shrink to become so unseen and meaningless. But why?

I am calling for you to step up and find your place! You belong to those incredible networks of connections. Your role is central; if only you could see it, your receiving channel, and find yourself in the middle.

In other words, your strategy is to become an energetic match to all those transactions until you find yourself in the center and instrumental in making them happen. A spirited match comes from your alignment with that reality and finding how you belong to it.

I have been in the financial world for over twenty years, structuring hundreds of millions of dollars of bonds, funds, and transactions. It was so exciting. I loved every part of it—the challenges, the level of impact, and the sophistication of it all!

It felt aligned and normal because these transactions meant creating more growth and development for thriving sectors, communities, regions, and countries. And that felt like the most beautiful mission to carry out!

My strategy aligned with my fundamentals: to help women create as much wealth as possible, feel free and empowered, and spread it to the world. It is about becoming a channel for receiving money and wealth, living a life of freedom of choice, and helping how it spreads beyond business. My role as a mentor and business strategist, launching different programs and working with incredible women worldwide, is stunning others.

Why would it be hard for us to create wealth and easy for them? They refer to those who know how to make money.

WHAT WILL BE YOUR STRATEGY FOR WEALTH CREATION?

Creating wealth is accessible to everyone. It starts by setting up a business strategy and focusing on providing the best service to your clients. You get compensated for the excellence of your service and the need for what you do.

It doesn't matter where you are or what you have done before. You can shift your mindset and become aligned with wealth. Creating wealth is about being aligned with the frequency of wealth and becoming a match for it. That is the strategy you want to elaborate on for yourself.

Even if you don't have a precise business, work on your inner beliefs and attitude to start preparing to open the receiving channel. No one will give you your worth; there will not be one person who will provide you with that. It will come to you from different places. It takes realignment with what you genuinely want and connecting with your inner force to truly appreciate how much you deserve to live your best life and make your dream a reality.

Sometimes, it may feel so far away and so inaccessible!

It is all in the mind, and that needs to change. It is time to create a new identity that aligns with your goals. People cannot become who they want to be because they get too attached to their identity and what they want.

You see the shift happening more easily for people who have hit rock bottom. Do you know why?

For two simple and intuitive reasons. Because at that moment, you are willing to let go of everything and everyone to pull yourself out of survival mode. Undeniably, you must rescue yourself first, which is when the shift happens.

The second reason is that when you are at the lowest point, you will realize that you are still okay even if you have been frightened and scared. Even if those images still haunt you. You are still OK. Breathing and enjoying the miracle of life—if only you could see it. When you connect with the tiniest light you could find, or you could still touch, you will grow.

This is your choice to make!

This book shows you that you do not need to reach rock bottom for it to happen. You can start now in whatever phase of your life cycle you find yourself in. Doing it code by code helps you structure your steps, and building from your strategic context creates a solid foundation.

MAKE YOUR WHY BIG

It all starts by defining your mission. This step helps you create the vital context you need as your mission develops into your WHY. The bigger the WHY, the more straightforward and accessible the HOW will seem!

Focusing on the WHY and acting toward it will help the HOW unfold.

Leading with purpose is a powerful way for female leaders to make a lasting impact and inspire their teams. Here are some strategies to help you define your mission and encourage others to follow your vision:

- **Clarify Your Purpose:** Reflect on your values and what truly matters. What drives you as a leader? What impact do you want on your team, organization, or the world? Defining your purpose is the first step in leading with intention.

- **Set Clear Goals:** Establish specific, measurable, achievable, relevant, and time-bound (SMART) goals that align with your purpose. These goals guide your actions and help you stay on track toward your mission.
- **Communicate Your Vision**: Clearly articulate your purpose and vision to your team and stakeholders. Use compelling storytelling to convey why your mission matters and how it will benefit others. Show people the broader significance of your goals to engage their emotions.
- **Lead by Example:** Demonstrate your commitment to your purpose through your actions. Your behavior should be consistent with your values and vision. When your team sees your dedication, they are more likely to follow suit.
- **Foster a Collaborative Environment**: Encourage open dialogue and collaboration within your team. Create a safe space where team members feel comfortable sharing and aligning their ideas with the broader purpose.
- **Delegate and Empower:** Trust your team to contribute to fulfilling your mission. Empower team members by delegating responsibilities and encouraging them to take ownership of their work. Recognize and reward their contributions.
- **Support Development**: Invest in your team members' growth and development. Provide training, mentorship, and skill-building opportunities that align with your purpose. Helping your team members grow is a part of your mission and a way to create a more capable and engaged team.
- **Celebrate Milestones:** Recognize and celebrate achievements and milestones that contribute to your purpose. Acknowledging the progress made toward your vision reinforces the significance of your mission and motivates your team.
- **Adapt and Innovate**: Be flexible and open to change. As circumstances evolve, your mission may require adjustments. Embrace innovation and adapt your strategies to stay aligned with your evolving purpose.

- **Seek Feedback:** Encourage honest feedback from your team and stakeholders. Constructive criticism can help refine your approach, ensuring your mission remains relevant and practical.
- **Network and Collaborate:** Connect with like-minded leaders and organizations that share your purpose. Collaborative efforts can amplify your impact and help you reach broader audiences.
- **Stay Resilient:** Leading with purpose can be challenging, and you may encounter obstacles and setbacks. Maintain resilience, perseverance, and a positive mindset to overcome challenges and stay focused on your mission.
- **Lead with Empathy:** Understand your team members' needs and concerns. Show empathy by actively listening and addressing their worries, and demonstrate your commitment to their well-being.

Leading with purpose is about achieving personal success and positively impacting the world. Your mission can be a driving force that inspires and empowers your team to achieve greatness while making a difference in the lives of others. By staying true to your purpose and following these strategies, you can lead authentically and leave a lasting legacy.

ACTIVITY FOR CODE 5

D efine the context of this new chapter of your life and layer it over your previous one.

My context for this year is _____

Pile it on top of your previous contexts.

For N-1 _____

For N-2 _____

If you had the best strategy, what would you like to achieve?

_____

_____

_____

_____

What is your highest vision for your life?

_____
_____
_____
_____

Connect with the different identities you have inside of you. Write them here.

_____
_____
_____
_____

How will you use your different identities to let your gift emerge and turn your vision into reality?

_____
_____
_____
_____

Define your context for this new chapter of your life and layer it on top of your previous one.

HEALING

I journaled for days and days. I kept writing my mantras. I had different ones to change my whole belief system—to shift myself from an energy of lack and a negative state of mind I felt locked in.

There were days when I believed "that I am happy and grateful that money comes to me from different sources continuously," and I saw it happening. There were days when I wrote and repeated: "I am happy and grateful that I win and prosper wherever I go," and I witnessed incredible things unfolding from nowhere. And there were days I needed so badly to feel that "I am happy and grateful that I attract only love, appreciation and respect."

What a journey it is. One that keeps you so busy with yourself that you can get lost in your journaling forever. Day after day, I had growing emotions and feelings that "everything is going to be okay." I want you to integrate this statement first. Make it the number one shift to the software in your subconscious mind.

Any trauma leaves sequels that create roots holding you so tight it makes you suffocate by yourself. Feeling breathless, anxious, stressed, and lost in an ocean of bitterness, rage, and shame for yourself. Year after year, you become acquainted with those wounds, which become your identity and emotional home. When those emotional habits anchor deeply, it is hard to change them, but it is not impossible.

It took me journaling with discipline and intentional thinking for hundreds of days of reprogramming, re-believing, and remodeling my subconscious mind to know that wealth, joy, and peace of mind are all possible. I did skip a few days during those three years of introspection, but I kept going. Our company is back to structuring and closing multiple seven and 8-figure transactions to make this concept incredibly potent and authentic. I am providing many proofs of concept about how those codes, when followed, will lift you to a field I did not know was possible to get the keys to. I saw it happening to my clients first and even faster than for me.

You only need consistency, discipline and perseverance to keep yourself on track.

CODE 6
DISCIPLINE YOURSELF

E very change and transformation you bring into your life correlates with your capacity to discipline yourself. That discipline is not only about taking action and doing it repeatedly. It is about your intentionality in reprogramming your mind and helping you shift your paradigm by establishing new internal software to help you align with the frequency of what you want to see in your life.

Discipline may need to be enforced initially by a mentor, a friend or a family member. Nevertheless, when it comes to your personal development and inner transformation, the decision starts with you. The existing tools can help you achieve your goals and strengthen your inner game. You need motivation and inspiration to start, but only discipline gets you moving forward and helps you keep the excitement.

DISCIPLINE CREATES CHAMPIONS

Even if no results are happening yet, the discipline mirrors your dedication. It keeps you on track and helps you stay focused. When you watch athletes, they are who they are because of their discipline. And their discipline didn't come in the last months before becoming champions and winners. Their discipline started at an early age. They were programmed that way because of a parent, a coach, or their unforgettable drive. Will Smith's movie King Richard showed how he trained his two girls, Serena and Venus William, to become the most prominent tennis legend. He taught them with rigorous discipline. Rain or shine, they were on the tennis court every day, playing, strengthening their game, building their muscle, and conditioning their state of mind. He believed, and they believed. Their story was not theirs anymore. They represent every young girl who wants to think and create a legendary life.

They were inspired, encouraged, and, of course, disciplined—day after day. Results don't come easy, and results don't come fast. They take time. They test you. They crush you and may knock you down. It is up to you to stand back up and return with discipline. Walk with your head up because you are legendary the moment you decide and the moment you integrate discipline as part of who you are.

The same thing applies to any field, for absolutely anyone. The attitude of a champion depends on your ability to maintain discipline. The first thing I do in my programs for leadership, success, and wealth creation is to set up a morning routine. Some women trust the BAL method mentorship so much they do it without missing one day. Going through every step of the process, understanding how all the results we have today are not matching what we want; they come because of an old paradigm that needs shifting and reprogramming. The only way to achieve that is through discipline and intentionality. Discipline combined with intentionality makes you reach new heights.

I saw it over and over. The women we celebrate for their fast change and for spreading inspiration and unexpected opportunity are the most disciplined ones. We can have the dedication and the will to change, but without the tools, it remains wishful thinking. When you get the tools but take them for granted without putting in the time and effort to build success habits, it does not matter how much you invest in yourself.

Bringing in a New Mantra

The hardest part when starting something is keeping it up and maintaining the journey. That comes with discipline. Discipline does not mean doing great things every day. There could be a day when you might feel like you are not moving at all, but the fact that you put yourself back into the energetics of where you are going and the dedication to make it work counts as a continuity of momentum. Minor action counts, as small as repeating to yourself a well-selected mantra, like "I attract love, respect and magic money." This statement becomes our new mantra as new codes unfold through this book, and as you put words on the level of vibrations, I want you to align with it for yourself, your family, the work you do, and the legacy you want to leave behind.

Do It With Intentionality and Focus

Discipline goes beyond taking action. It is about becoming intentional about what you do and think about. You do not want to waste time thinking about the past, the problems, and what makes you worry. Taking any direction in your thinking will compound with all the thoughts that pile up on top of each other. Being intentional is shifting your mind to think about what you want to see compound in a positive direction. Each time, when the worries and the hint of things not working out or getting worse come back to haunt you, stop it! Strengthen yourself and stop the thoughts from pulling you down to more negativity.

Instead, you should focus on your objectives, improving your skills to become undeniably good at what you do and creating your brand.

It takes real focus when you decide to change your life after realizing that you have nothing to lose and much to gain from winning the bet.

It is similar to making a promise to yourself and your loved ones.

So this is what I did: I made a promise to myself, my children and every woman going through any tough time of struggle, frustration or setback. My commitment was so deep that it overrode everything else. I stopped caring about how to do it and made the why so big. It cleared the road.

When you do that, you plant that promise in your heart, letting it guide you and watering it daily with the correct energies. It will enlighten you with discipline and consistency. In addition, keep your intellectual, scientific and logical mind alert. You can only maintain this combination with discipline.

You got this. So strengthen your belief in it. A caterpillar never leaves the cocoon too early because it thinks it won't work out or something is wrong with itself. A caterpillar will turn into the most beautiful butterfly, no matter how dark and long the journey could be.

Keeping the void is about focusing on the prize, even though every message screams otherwise. Even if events do not match your expectations or you don't see any results, remember that it takes time to let go of negative thoughts and habits before you can restore purity.

How Do You Stay Focused?

The big question frequently asked is, "How do you stay focused when you have many things happening around you?"

As a mother or a person responsible for family members and close friends, there are many elements to remember. As a CEO, I have so many numbers to compute over and over. As a Leader, there will always be so many new ideas to organize and plan and challenges to be ready to face. In addition to focus, other questions asked are, "How do you keep calm?" and "How do you stay grounded through it all?"

I used to think it was about planning and respecting a tight schedule. But with time, it became more about trusting that things will always work out so that you can juggle many responsibilities while feeling at peace.

Letting go of the fear of not being enough in those roles and responsibilities. Be fully present in every aspect of your life. Give it your all and keep a real focus on every task you do. Trust that the rest will be okay.

What is incredible, although it may appear counter-intuitive. This way of being will give you more time and freedom. When we focus on what we do, our productivity multiplies—and we need less time than what we originally put aside. Focus makes you connect with the moment and get anchored through your senses. You will know what you are doing and what you are feeling. This way, you will remember every detail.

When you focus, you don't need to return to your notes to

remember anything. You listen to what people tell you, immersing yourself fully in their story like a movie. Connecting with your emotions helps you understand and feel whatever there is to feel there. You can call it the sixth sense. I call it being present, focused, and fully alive.

Finally, giving time to everything you do will connect you with the moment and help you appreciate more what you do and who you are doing what you do. It brings a sweeping feeling of appreciation for every finished task. This creates a smooth shift toward a positive mindset, enhancing your focus and outlook.

EVEN WITH DISCIPLINE, BE STRATEGIC

Discipline has to be strategic, mainly when improving one's skills and understanding of the subject of focus.

If it is just to accumulate knowledge for the sake of it, you deserve the medal of recognition today. Because–trust me–with all the knowledge you have, you are a walking encyclopedia. But will it change you from within? Will it upgrade your game and magnetize the results you want to receive in your life? It takes more than just absorbing information, reading and watching videos. Self-development is walking the talk and doing the work, applying it to your life so that it becomes an integral part of you.

When you can also stop occasionally and think about what you will do with the knowledge, you start to contemplate your life and everything about you. This is when you start integrating all of it into your being so that it becomes you. You will speak the part and communicate eloquently, and your confidence will flourish.

Otherwise, you could listen to thousands of videos and read hundreds of books. What counts is what you do with it. You want to roll up your sleeves and become a natural athlete, disciplined while taking action strategically. You need to know where you are going. It's not a train you take to Lala land. It is a train you ride to reach your specific dreams with a clear destination while being in perfect alignment with the depth of your soul.

You will feel elevated by owning and integrating the knowledge you have absorbed and using it to build your puzzle of excellence, expertise, services and products. Only then will you be poised to contribute and create a true impact using your genius, creativity and talent.

So, our brains are all the same. We are all structured the same way, just like the wealthiest people in the world or any average person walking in the street. What differentiates us are our paradigm and subconscious beliefs. Removing them is difficult, but you can reprogram them with discipline. They are not easy to alter, but integrating these codes will get you disciplined and dedicated to shifting your paradigm.

As you read this book, you will feel some of the limiting beliefs will dissipate and anything you inherited and allowed it to sink in. If you are truly ready to become a better version of yourself, ready to think and grow rich*, you need to make the code of discipline your priority. You become unstoppable as you get on track to move yourself to the next level of results.

The Secret is to Never Give Up

Creating success and wealth is a challenging journey. It doesn't feel like riding a musical train at Disney World. It can be tricky, painful, long, lonely, and at times. The secret is never to give up. And the how is the million-dollar question.

You need to retreat inside you when it gets too hard to handle or be. What you retrieve inside of you is resilience, strength, and fortitude. What happens at that moment is that, on the vibration scale, you are at the lowest or the bottom and rising feels immense, bemusing, and seemingly impossible. I have been there. I know what it is. That's when you hold on to that most minor light you can see. It could be just a plant you watch change daily or your child growing more confident. It can be a song you start loving or a "never give up" quote you grow understanding more each day. You can also choose to find expertise so you can begin to master little by little every day. That progress is you being reborn. Progress is you emerging like a phoenix from the ashes. Use the deepest pain and the most formidable challenges to empower you to grow into your highest self.

---

* Napoleon Hill, Think and Grow Rich (TarcherPerigee, 2007)

By being amid these incredible ladies inside our masterminds and group programs, I grew to love the feeling of helping and serving. The role I was in made me feel valuable and valued. It was a way for me to think that I matter, reconnect with my mission more, and embody it. I also grew, matured and powered up daily as I thought this was my destiny. All is possible because I deeply believe in the infinite power of the divine and that everything happens for a reason.

During the two years, I felt stuck; I couldn't see the wisdom from the moment's bitterness. Today, I know, in hindsight, that this was feed-back from the universe because I had a more significant calling. Becoming a voice for women brings a thrill I could not have discovered without going through pain, reaching rock bottom, and pushing myself up again. I know what it is to be hurt, betrayed, and lose everything you've ever worked for–which helps me connect more with people.

CREATE YOUR ROADMAP TO SUCCESS

You can create your own recipe and success roadmap by integrating the lessons learned and using all the inspiring stories you encounter on your path. The BAL Method is an incredible recipe*; you could use it as you craft your own. It has worked for me and hundreds of women to date. Many felt stuck in daily habits and frustrated that the day was too short to complete everything they had planned.

When you are a visionary person and want to impact the lives of multiple people with your business, you will be juggling so many things at once. There will also be frustration when things seem chaotic or out of control. You need to understand that your state dictates the results you create for yourself daily. To be successful, you cannot be operating out of a place of frustration. And to achieve the frequency of success, you need to trust the creation and business growth process. As nothing happens overnight, your job is to keep a success mindset throughout the journey.

We all function with energy. This is why you need to clear yourself from all the energies not serving you, from past mistakes, failures,

---

* www.balmethod.com/digital

setbacks, and anything that didn't go how you wanted. Start honoring yourself and standing for your word as if it was law. In practical terms, your most important objective is to seek excellence in your expertise by pushing yourself to become greater tomorrow in what you do than how you are today. In addition, honoring yourself means treating yourself with respect and consideration. This is how you would work on your self-image to build a strong belief about your success and how you deserve the best.

Finally, have faith despite the obstacles and the struggles, and trust your intuition and the power inside of you to guide you in reaching the success you seek. Make up your mind, shift your attitude, and seek success and excellence because you deserve the best life.

Get into the habit of cheering yourself up while magnetizing what you want to have as an actual reality in your life. Join me in spreading a beautiful Mantra: **"I attract Love, Respect, and Magic Money always... always."**

Let love feed your soul and fuel all the courage you need to achieve your wildest dreams. Use respect to protect your soul, enforce your boundaries and build an energetic shield around your inner light. Be ready to receive money, have all the choices in your hands, and create the best life for yourself, your children, your loved ones, and the world.

Love will spread, respect will spread, and money will create an impact. Together, we can change the world by changing ourselves and our beliefs. Let's align on all of this!

Case Study from the Global Mastermind Community

Discipline changes everything in your relationship with yourself as it helps you boost your confidence about your ability to do what you set yourself to achieve. It is truly a privilege to watch the impact of the Believe-Act-Lead* Method inside our program by seeing how it helped women leap into a higher version of themselves. Just like Lara launched her new old jeans recycling brand after the enormous impact of the

---

*   https://www.amazon.com/dp/B0BKGW1667

pandemic on her Communication Agency. Similarly, after regaining confidence and honoring herself with respect, love, and appreciation, Sandra was nominated as a board member in a large, international financial institution. Daily work and a morning routine proved incredibly efficient. After two years of health struggles, Firdaous also got a high-level executive position at a global investment bank in London.

I want to add another incredible story that surprised me through the swift transformation. When Nina joined the French 6-month program, she was a real estate developer whose business took an enormous toll due to COVID-19. She didn't like anything about her life anymore. We started working together in October, focusing on the first phase of the BAL Method, which is mindset and energetics. I was amazed and in admiration of her trust and discipline. We focused all our energy on her elevation. Nina discovered a new passion as a designer of revived traditional Kaftan, a love she inherited from her mother and never got around to making a reality. The more she started believing in the possibility and potentialities of that significant shift, the more she became creative and inspired. In February, she organized the first private sale of her beautiful and newly created collection. We worked on her strategy, branding, the name and the positioning and something so beautiful was born, making her reach six figures within four months into the program. Discipline can bring you fulfillment, success and wealth.

Discipline brings you freedom in every facet of your life!

ACTIVITY FOR CODE 6

With consistent discipline, you can move a mountain!

To conclude this code, this is an invitation to write your Mantra, the one you want to live by and absorb as your new truth.

Consistency and a disciplined repetition of your mantra reprogram your subconscious mind. Here are a few that worked wonders for me and my clients:

> *"I am happy and grateful that money continuously comes
>   to me from different sources."*
> *"I win and prosper wherever I go."*
> *"Everything is going to be okay."*
> *"I attract only love and respect."*
> And my latest one:
> *"I attract love, respect and magic money."*

Choose the mantra that feels wholly aligned with your goals and write it six times.

_____

_____

_____

_____

Get started today!

CONNECTION

I used to hide from the media and the press. I grew up wanting to be discrete and humble—and then I found the need to bring my voice forward and to be the one to talk about female leadership, starting with who I am and what I am about. I don't know if I chose to become a public figure. I think it is more my journey that drove me to it. As a leader, there is no time to sit back and hide if you want to keep the momentum and continue on your path. The journey I had set forth the day my parents let me study abroad when I was nineteen came rushing back when I found myself drifting away from the fundamentals of why I am who I am. This summer brought all of it full circle. It felt like an astrological readjustment putting me back into the restart point again with more potent energetics.

I turned to social media to get inspiration when I was at my lowest point because I needed a reassuring voice. I was looking for evidence-however, that might be that everything will be okay. I listened to music on loops. I put on Beyonce's "Listen, listen to the voice I have inside" over and over to infiltrate the deepest parts of my body and soul. I repeated songs, and I felt connected to a zone. I found comfort in "Calling You" by Outlandish and Baghdad Café's "I'm Calling You."

I was calling the infinite intelligence, the divine power, mother nature, the "above it all." I wanted my voice to be heard so far beyond the three-dimensional space I found myself in, suffocated by all the stress, difficulties, challenges, and problems... it was tough!

I turned to the light above all of us, the more immense power and believed it with all of my strength. I started sensing that love was out there; there was respect and relief. All the wisdom was hard to see from lessons that took so much out of me with the hurt and the pain that came with it. I was not sure I could. But I believed. I disciplined myself with every inch of my body. I pulled myself up, tiny bit by tiny bit and connected with the slightest light inside—a light of gratefulness for breathing and feeling the sun on my skin. I created a safety net with the closeness of nature. I saw it compounded with my children's love, and I persevered when clients started to celebrate their success before I could truly escape from it all.

I poured so much love and dedication into my brand, my experience, my story and the connections I made through social media, including mentors, friends and beautiful clients.

I am so grateful for everything this digital era is offering. It allows us to connect with the whole world, feel alive again, believe again and even make millions if we choose to.

CODE 7
MAKE EXCELLENT YOUR BRAND

The most successful entrepreneurs started from nothing. They worked hard, persevered to reach their goals, and made sacrifices. Their families made sacrifices for them to acquire the proper education and help them achieve financial freedom and respect. Everything becomes possible when you stay focused, work hard, and have a good education.

In my work on women's empowerment and leadership, the most important thing is to gain the power and courage to enter the decision-making sphere. You have the ability and all it takes to transform the world. It is a crucial affirmation that every woman needs to remember to thrive and inspire the next generation. Your job is to become a role model for every young girl and woman.

Not only does working hard come from childhood but confidence is also rooted in the first years of life. Good things don't come effortlessly just by a spell. You need to have the right mindset, great discipline, and perseverance at all times. More importantly, we should not be afraid to lose and take on risks and challenges. The only way to succeed is by getting ready to take on risks, developing resilience through failure, and standing back up again no matter what.

A strong mindset, a deep belief in reaching your goals and professional success, and hard work will pave the way to excellence.

What Makes You a Brand?

Yes, excellence is the brand you want to have. But don't confuse it with being good at everything or even perfect before starting anything. You want to get started so that you can become good at it.

As women, the world taught us that the only way to navigate a male-dominated professional world was to work harder, be more creative, get better results, and always show up perfect. When you reach a high-level leadership position and become a board member for a large corporation, you not only carry hope for everyone but also represent all those who could not make it. You know who you are, where you belong and where you come from. You also know how long and challenging the journey was to get there.

This is why the first step to success is clarifying what you want to become. A clear vision for your goals and objectives is necessary to reach fulfillment and success in your professional and personal life. In that regard, Oprah Winfrey is the perfect role model for all women worldwide, spreading motivation and inspiration. Oprah shines through her firm conviction: "You don't get what you wish for, you don't get what you hope for, you get what you strongly believe in." Thus, visualizing what you want to reach by articulating your dreams and ambitions sets the tone for what type of success you will achieve. Keeping the vision will strengthen your belief in it.

A strong belief in achievable goals will take a long way to reach them. You will grow a robust inner power to be able to overcome the obstacles and all the challenges on the road to success. You will learn to shut down any little voice telling you the opposite.

You are responsible for what happens to you. Taking responsibility for your destiny can significantly leap you towards success and fulfillment. When your goal is vivid about having a life full of happiness and abundance combined with a solid and deep belief that you deserve such a life, you will see it materialize.

Excellence Makes You Stand Out

Everyone wants to be famous, and people admire others for being famous. The only thing is that fame fades away, and what stays on is the service rendered. As Martin Luther King rightly expressed, "Not everybody can be famous, but everybody can be great because greatness is determined by service." This is one of my favorite quotes in my previous book, Believe Act Lead. I am applying it differently here.

When you know your goal, you will find the perfect service you can provide and get well paid for it. And for long-lasting success from your service, you have to be the best at it. This way, it becomes challenging to replace you as you confirm your position as an authority, a leader, and an expert. By providing the best service, you get a fulfilling satisfaction from changing people's lives. You will keep distinguishing yourself through your excellence by raising yourself to the top. At the top, there is no competition!

But with success comes hatred, jealousy, and cruelty. All these negative energies could affect you if you let them get to you. It is essential to master navigating through all these energies without letting them impact your inside and change your behavior.

Unfortunately, the closest family and social circle will not always be happy for your success. You might get labeled arrogant and selfish. On the one hand, you become perceived as egotistical because your leadership might make you sound contemptuous. On the other hand, they consider you selfish because you did not take everyone with you towards the same success—like if you had a boat and everybody needed to be in it. Even if you have always been generous and helped whenever you can, the appreciation will never be the same way ever again. You need to be ready for that. An impressive range of detractors and attackers may appear. Beware.

The best response is to aim for excellence and to become the most outstanding expert you can be!

Yes, excellence should be your brand. It will be the best response you could give to injustice, attacks, and toxic people around you. And above all, excellence is the best gift you can give to yourself.

Finally, success correlates with who you surround yourself with—

choose positive and like-minded people. Network with people who can help you achieve that excellence and bring out the very best in you!

This is Your Time!

We have started a modern business era where everyone can become a self-made legend and star. This is your time!

Unleash the leader inside. Let that leader shine in the spotlight of your stage—the stage you want to create so that you can shape your brand and let it shine for you. A brand can grow universal in no time, elevating you to the status of a legend—the one that lives beyond who you are and what you do. Your impact and those of whoever you have impacted create a ripple effect.

We are so lucky to live in this digital era. The world has opened the door for you to craft your mark and leave a legacy behind. It is the time when you can create a media platform and connect with millions worldwide by consistently showing up.

This code will make your brand shine and magnetize your dream goals. Sit back and enjoy watching your leadership rise!

Create Your Stage and Let Your Brand Shine

I used to think that the more discreet you are about your work and your achievements, the more humble and considerate you will appear to others. These are values we grow up with, and that spread all around the world.

It's time to anchor a new paradigm around the subject. The biggest brands and institutions don't wait for someone to come and talk about them, praise them, or even present them. They build their channel to educate people about what they do and insist on being the leaders in their field. The World Bank* has built a whole structure around setting up conferences and stages for stakeholders, representatives and different people to come and talk about their projects and initiatives. It is such a privilege to be included in their Spring Meetings, their Annual Meet-

---

*   www.worldbank.org

or their marketplace, where development projects can get a few minutes and a little space to showcase their impact and get all the chances beside them to find the right partner, the right investor and the right mentor.

Similarly, the World Economic Forum* (WEF) had become an institution on its own, creating its stage, promoting its work and becoming a whole media. They do not rely on others to promote them. The WEF meetings in Davos † became the most sought-after event for corporations, the private and public sectors, and philanthropic and thought leaders. It is the meeting everyone in business wants to join. Sponsoring, enrolling, participating, and becoming a member costs money. They have built a stand-alone structure and "a must" event to connect with. It did not happen the first year, but they were visionary when they decided to grab the center of attention in Davos. Every entrepreneur vision board has a moment where we sit on the white chair with the last name tag and share our story with the world.

No one will come and choose you to become the great YOU. You must decide for yourself and keep that vision and that position forever and against all odds.

We are born into this digital era for a reason. That reason is not to align with the old "hide and be discreet" paradigm anymore or to "wait until someone finds you."

Time is passing, and everyone will always be busy with their life. It is all up to you. Your decision to make. Your actions to take. Get started today. Building a lasting brand doesn't usually happen in just a few weeks or months. It could take two to three years before standing out as a thought leader, a reference, and a true legend. You want to get busy creating your stage because you can because you are here for a reason and because you have a profound mission to fulfill. Review Code 5 about your strategic context to find your mission and why again.

There is a legend and a star inside each one of us. We cut it short before we give it the chance to be. You will be surprised by how extraordinary the star in you is. Please provide that legendary star in you this chance.

---

* https://www.weforum.org/about/world-economic-forum
† https://www.weforum.org/events/world-economic-forum-annual-meeting-2024

Use your voice. Use your talent. Use your genius. And step up into the spotlight!

Do it with the excellence you have inside. Excellence is the best of what you have. The best that you can give. Again, we are talking about something other than perfection. We are talking about your best. Perfection will stop short because perfection can never equate to your best. Perfection means keeping a certain level so that everything looks in order. It will make you stop shorter than if you give yourself the right and the ability to push yourself further. Seeking perfection limits yourself by reflecting what society and people see as perfection. Let go, focus on giving your best, and be proud of your best in everything you do. This is what excellence should mean to you.

The Meaning of Self-promotion

Throughout history, gaining recognition has never been easier than it is now. Things were different before. To become a star or a celebrity, you had to be chosen by an agent or an organization. Any aspiring star needed to go through a filter and a selection process. Then, it came with many conditions so that you could fit the mold for your chosen role.

Today, no one needs to choose you or validate your decision about your worthiness. You get to decide that you are the one, how you want others to see you and what you stand for. You get to create a brand that precisely reflects who you are. All you need to do is improve your skills and strengthen your human side and all its needs. Because that human side is the one that holds you up to ensure your desire is alive. Your role is to empower the human in you while building your brand and allowing people to see you through your chosen platform.

The more aligned you are with your beliefs and reality, the more unshakable you will grow as you become more known. The alignment will draw people to you because of your message and how they feel about it. The level of exposure you are ready for is what you will attract in your life. You could be the most hidden secret and continue feeling unseen, or take action and be okay with self-promotion. When you shy away from being seen, you shut the door off to your brand, making it to the surface and attracting clients to reach the level of success and wealth you seek.

MAKE SOCIAL MEDIA YOUR OWN MEDIA OUTLET

Social Media is the open door to your digital presence. Every day, a billion USD is spent on e-learning and more on products and other services. Digital courses and training will reach a trillion USD by 2032. This new marketplace is different from what it used to be, all on the internet and social media.

You need to create a solid digital presence to be part of the trend and the new way of doing business. And social media has made it accessible to everyone. However, we all agree that social media is busy. You can focus on the competition and the tiny space for anyone else. Or you can grab the opportunity with open arms and pave your way to stand out as a Trademark.

First, let's clarify some simple facts about social media. Your social media is not your business; it is the media platform you use for your business. It is an interactive business card that helps you present yourself and your company while interacting with whoever sees it. When you master it and become good at it, you can grow your business through it.

When you create your brand using social media, the objective is not to look like someone else but to create an outlet—like a magazine—that mirrors who you are.

When I started in the digital world, I wanted my brand to feel elegant and inspiring. I also wanted it to breathe advanced knowledge, information, and excellence. I had never used social media before, so I avoided it. But for the past three years, I have used it as my outlet to share stories, events, and programs, invite incredible female leaders as guests in the Women's Empowerment Series* and join our BAL Method Masterminds and programs.

I use social media (LinkedIn, Facebook and Instagram, as well as Youtube) as my diary to pencil down the work I do as I am writing new articles, a new book—and also some behind-the-scenes as a mother and

---

* https://www.youtube.com/channel/UCQdse3sRgnO2ioFXVS6dmJQ

a mentor and strategist. The behind-the-scenes gets usually more inter-
action. It gives access to some parts of your personality through which
many people relate to you. People connect with others through social
aspects. In our differences, we are the same in many ways, and we relate
to each other through our stories at different levels.

Social media shouldn't feel like pressure for you to find the right
thing to talk about so that you can please whoever might be reading. It
should be about clarifying your message about the work you do. For
example, you can share new programs and invite new clients to join
when the doors are open for your programs, the service you provide, or
the products you sell.

It is a way for people to understand what you do and articulate the
different facets of your mission and work. It is not meant to be perfect
but rather to reflect the evolution and growth of your business and your
presence as a public figure. It is about creating connections and interactions with incredible people worldwide.

What matters is for you to create new connections as they happen
one at a time and to feel that you have something to say that day, something to share, something to inspire and give hope to someone else.

It is meant to be simple and becomes simple when approached
easily. You can just make someone feel good by sharing your joy or
feeding them the words, "You are amazing the way you are. Keep going.
You are doing great, and you will get there." These are the simplest of
messages we all need to hear.

Start with what helps you, what you want to hear, and what message
you want to send. Then, build on it!

It is about progression and improvement. You will witness it firsthand as you create, write, and design graphics representing you and your
work. Find the branding that mirrors who you are and what you feel at
that moment.

It is a journey of creating and building brick by brick, which, with
the right attitude, will turn into a masterpiece.

ARTICULATE YOUR MESSAGES CLEARLY

You want to use messages that are clear, true and honest. There is no pretending that would ever get you anywhere. Fake it till you make it is not about lying; it is about reprogramming yourself to greatness and embarking on your journey for it to become the story you tell in hindsight.

Articulating a clear message will shift your business to new heights. You want to create a brand for people to connect with you. Thus, there are three essential things you want to make sure you have in any post you write or article you share and in every communication you make:

- Be relevant,
- Be relatable,
- Be consistent.

The first one is the very reason why you write, and you share your messages. It has to be relevant. The second one is to show that you are not a robot and not a distant leader; you don't want people to put you on a pedestal and feel so far away from you. Finally, being consistent is the most essential point of all. Being consistent is connected to Code 6 about discipline. Discipline makes the difference between those who are genuine and aligned with their truth and those who cannot keep it up. The more consistent you are, the more credible you will be.

In addition, to create authentic connections, besides consistency and credibility, you want to be genuinely committed to your work and your role as a leader in your field. The impact will be remembered when the message is straightforward. The most sophisticated experts in the world are who they are because of their ability to speak the most complicated concepts so simply that my six-year-old Zahraty can understand them. Ultimately, you want to aim for this in your writing and messaging.

It is not about using the most complicated and sophisticated words that impress us with who you are and your work. It is the simplicity of it all. Our brain wants to save calories and avoid headaches by guessing what you say. Be simple, choose simple and think simple. There is power in simplicity to create lasting connections. They need to be simple and easy, one at a time.

We are in a new era of business, where you get to have it all—transforming your life into the most extraordinary journey and connecting with thousands and millions of people. People are doing incredible things. To get started, all you need is the courage to share your story and use straightforward messages to everyone.

When you want a life beyond your dreams, create a story and share it to inspire people. When you share your story, what matters is what you unlock in the process and your ability to transfer the codes and keys you have channeled through your experience and for who you are. Share your story and share the information from your heart. It will land at the right place. We all crave connections. Be the one to create them with love and care—one at a time. You can then transform your business to reach multi-million levels.

You have it in you to build a World-Class brand that genuinely represents who you are. Let the legend in you rise!

BECOME A TRADEMARK

My whole life, I have worked hard, sought excellence, and given my best in whatever I am doing. As a daughter, a sister, a student, a graduate, a researcher, a professor, an executive, a professional, a wife, and a mother, I have worn different hats and juggled different roles. I keep a smile, keep faith, and always believe in a better future for me, you, and all of us.

Early on, I knew I had an important role—a role more significant than myself, transcending frontiers and barriers. My role was to pave the way for young girls and women and to show them what was possible. My role was always to stand tall in a very man-dominated environment, in meetings where I was the only woman.

Today, my role is to be the Guide for every woman so she can celebrate herself every day for who she truly is and for her ability to magnetize the beauty of life to herself, create wealth and make a lasting impact. Thus, I profoundly believe every woman deserves to be celebrated for her bravery and grace!

This is all you need to take a leadership position through the work you do and through your understanding of the impact you make and the undeniable value you provide. I want you to claim it here because you know that your experience and your story have prepared you to become the leader you want to be and build all the success you deserve and the fulfillment you aspire to. You need to embody this to win in this game of leadership. You have a uniqueness to you; no one has gone through precisely the same experiences - the amazing ones, the not-so-good ones and particularly the challenging and demanding parts. No one can ever be you.

Every year you have gone through has its context, including all the memories and lessons. By stacking every year through its context one on top of the other, you will build the most powerful story of your life. This solid foundation is for you to use and rise higher in wealth creation, impact, and the legacy of everything you stand for.

Your presence on social media and digital platforms should mirror your everyday work and passion. Bring out the best version of yourself without sacrificing your most vulnerable, soft, and delicate side.

Stay assured that no one will ever be able to do what you do the same as you. You are incredible for who you are, and the world needs you for precisely who you are. Let the world see you. You are a Trademark.

If you want to start building a world-class brand everyone will remember, be the one to create it and claim your trademark. Otherwise, someone else will, and it won't be yours.

Case Study from the Global Mastermind Community

Code Seven brought so many successful stories to those inside our programs. After clarifying the messages, Linda could attract multiple six-figure investors in her innovative e-commerce startup. Amira received a nomination as a World Leader for her podcast about women's empowerment, and Maria quickly signed her first premium client.

ACTIVITY FOR CODE 7

L et's start thinking about what your branding will look like. What feelings do you want people to have when looking at your work and digital presence? Choose the correct description for you:

Elegant – Serious – Funny – Classy – Rock & Roll – Young – Polished – Wild – Natural – Fun – Luxury – Accessible – Comfort – Knowledge

_____

_____

_____

_____

What is your story that makes you so unique and so different:

_____

_____

_____

_____

Why is that?

_____

_____

_____

_____

How can you summarize that and extract your X factor?

_____

_____

_____

_____

I Always Felt Like an Artist

I have often been asked, "Why did you change your career?"

So I pause and wonder what they think is a change in my career. I never saw it that way. It has always been an elevation each time I moved somewhere else.

It was important to me to join an international financial institution at the beginning of my professional life. Then, I was ready for the role of economic advisor to the Prime Minister of Morocco for four years. After that, I swung between the public and private sectors because I appreciated their mutual importance and role in development and growth. This year, I am celebrating ten years into my entrepreneurship journey.

I had big dreams and goals I needed to reconnect with after a huge setback. They had become a blur. The challenges and the difficulties were all impressive and equalized the big dream I set myself for.

As an entrepreneur, you have two choices at those moments. You either give up because it is too complicated and get lost in feeling wrong about your options and everything about you, or you swallow it all. Then, find wisdom in the most profound and challenging moments and uplift yourself.

As an artist, you can craft your path with all the creativity in your body and add as many directions as you want. From an artistic perspective, the duality becomes more bearable, and you can even make sense of it. Embracing your life as an artist ignites your creativity and thrust for everything that comes because they help you craft your masterpiece.

Aren't we all artists in our own way?

This code is to find and use the artist inside you, letting others hear your voice. At that moment, you can watch the legendary version of you rise!

CODE 8
CREATE THE LEGEND

The eighth Code is my favorite. It's about creativity, recognizing the artist in you and becoming a Legend. We all have one. The creative, the artist, the little different side than the norms dictate. The Star. The wild and, at times, rebellious in you if only you allowed it to speak. The one that wants to say "no." The one who wants to try something different, unusual, maybe even a bit crazy. That will be like the panther–elegant yet smoothly dangerous.

You have that Legend who dreams of being free to express herself. The artist has what it takes to do something so unexpected just for the fun of it.

I often say if I had learned these codes earlier, I might be someone like Jennifer Lopez today. She embodies the roles of an artist, business-woman, and an inspiration for everyone to live life to the fullest while continuously evolving in colors, brands, and styles. Her life would be a surprise filled with love, luxury, and world-class experiences, creating a real impact.

Jennifer is not just an artist, singer, and actor; she is also an investor and an advocate for women's empowerment and celebrating being a woman. I deeply admire and resonate with her spirit, as she has risen to legendary status while remaining grounded in her humanity and cherishing the simple joys of being a mother and in love. Through the philanthropic venture Limitless Labs, she partnered with Goldman Sachs to provide Latin-owned small business startups access to capital. She also collaborated with nonprofits to loan Latina entrepreneurs $14 billion in loan capital.

This is an example of what it means to create wealth for you so that it can serve everyone else. You want to be an open channel for everything you can attract and receive. If each one of us did that, we would change the world altogether. I am such a firm believer in that. The path to contribution takes different forms, and being an artist in all its meaning is the overarching thread for the most part. Be an artist in your life, in your profession and your style. And become a legend in your field.

Feeling Like an Artist

In my previous book, Believe Act Lead, the driving thread was to embrace your life as your movie because you are the star. And as a star, you must let the artist in you create, innovate and amaze the world!

Looking at it through that lens, I see that my journey is one with a continuous theme of music playing from one scene to another and from one chapter to another in my life. I excelled throughout my youth as a pianist. I also loved ballet and classical dancing. My teacher once told my Mum that I was talented in classical dancing and I should pursue it as a career. As a scientist and math person, I would not entertain this, but it was flattering to come from a rigorous ballet teacher.

I loved dancing with all of my heart. I gave it all my soul and expression and felt it was my way of expressing my inner feelings. I could get lost in it and feel so good with the music—as if the universe heard me. It felt so good and recomforting from Salsa to Rock & Roll, to Tango and, of course, from my own culture's Belly Dancing. I had gotten so good at all of them at different stages in my life. With my sisters, we would spend the afternoons dancing away, laughing and enjoying every part of it.

I loved those moments; they shaped our childhood and made life fun, enjoyable, and fulfilling. We did not need anything from outside to make us feel alive. We knew how to feel alive from the inside. We were beautiful artists in our ways and enjoyed every piece of it.

We felt free to switch from one type of music to another. I played classical piano and many Chopin, Bach, Beethoven, and Mozart. In my youth, I received 14 years of rigorous piano training at the Conservatory of Piano in Casablanca, with exams and competitions at the end of the year. I am so proud to have received the Honorary diploma of the Conservatory. It took a lot of training, which I adored. We had a quarter queue piano growing up. I would open the windows to let the music flow and play a Chopin waltz or any entertaining piece. The neighbors could also enjoy the music; they loved that.

Fast-forward: My daughter Sarah does the same, although our house is more prominent. The piano is a Mahogany Steinway & Sons I bought in New York. I continued playing while working at the World Bank and studying at the Washington Conservatory of Music. It was an incredible phase because I revived my passion for piano and music. So, I brought those feel-good moments with movers when I moved back to Morocco.

Today, I listen to my 14-year-old Sarah playing Debussy's Arabesque or a Nocturne by Chopin, and I get a déjà-vu moment of me sitting on that Piano chair playing 30 years ago in my parents' house. Sarah loves to play and ensures that the whole house hears her, and even the neighbors, from afar, crossing the greens and the street. She opens the piano cover and pours her heart into playing, using the pedals to sustain the sound and let it resonate far and wide.

I am so grateful to witness the beauty transcending time and the love for music and life I can pass on to my children. Creating the most beautiful legacy involves sharing these values with future generations.

I am who I am because of the wild and untamed artist I have in me. The more I follow my heart, the more I see events unfolding in the most beautiful, harmonious way around me, like a perfect symphony. It comes by surrendering to the moment, without needing to control anything–trusting everything will unfold on its own and at the right time for them.

Throughout the day, I sing a song as if someone in another dimension set the theme. I don't think about it; I don't look for it; it just happens. It helps me create the most beautiful stories reflecting my real-time emotions on my social media pages—and I also use it to pour out so much writing and quotes that feel perfect for the moment and the circumstances.

Today, I bring music into everything I do, particularly inside our Leaders Mastermind, to enhance the vibes of the Module; it is the best compliment when we talk about emotional intelligence. I didn't realize how important this practice was until Dr. Pamela, a mentor-coach inside the Mastermind, mentioned it in her testimonial, saying how impactful the transformation was in helping her change her money story. I used music intuitively and connected different vibes to recreate new habits and overcome the blocking beliefs around money and other fears.

FIND HARMONY AROUND YOU

Look around and notice the harmony that surrounds you. Take a moment to feel the present. As we rush through many tasks during the day, we often miss out on so much.

We have only the present to impact the trajectory of our lives, so consider what you can do about it. In the present, you can think, feel, speak, or take action—those are your options. Each moment will become part of the past and will influence your future. Therefore, become more present and embrace the artist within you to accept every part of this experience.

Feeling the present moment brings you joy. Use all your senses and reconnect with yourself in every moment and every place. There are places we want to remember and situations we want to last forever. All of this happens because of how they make us feel and how we create a balance within ourselves.

The more intentional you are about feeling present, the more situations like that will appear in your life. Take a moment to look around and appreciate what you see. Admire and connect with nature, find harmony, and create memorable moments.

Today, as I become intentional about spreading beauty and magic, I am surrounded by all of it. When we travel, I prepare myself for beauty and magic. So we meet Jazz Bands in Harvard Square, encounter Ballet Performances in the street of South Beach, Miami, and find the Jasmine flowers waiting for us in Tunisia. The universe will bring all the magic you get ready to receive on your path. The more you see it in your daily habits and the simplicity of life, the more you magnetize greatness into your life.

Live your life as if you are an artist in a movie, an opera, a show, or a concert. If your life is a masterpiece, add the music that goes with it. Use where you are to make the most beautiful stage. In the most harrowing moments, let the bitterness and the sadness seem as attractive as any sad movie that made us all cry—like the movie "Love Story" or "The Thorn Birds." But we still loved every part of them.

When you show resilience and perseverance, everything you do will look incredible in hindsight. Take on your day as a story you will be sharing in hindsight. Make it through the odds and challenges with the best survival storyline in your mind.

Suppose your life was a movie. Be the Number ONE star of it and the source of creativity. Don't let someone else take your position. Be the STAR of yours!

APPROACH BUSINESS AS AN ART

I spent many years traveling the world as a World Bank official and later on as a Strategic Advisor, flying from country to country and going from meeting to meeting. Every time I was somewhere, I took a moment to feel the culture, understand the traditions, embrace the environment, and ground myself within all the colors and the vibes around me.

When I look back, the memories I carry with me are not those inside the meetings but the moments I was able to go for a walk in the streets of Hanoi in Vietnam or sit on a chair by the Mekong River to watch the sunset in Vientiane in Laos. I remember the feeling of watching the turtles on the beach in Bahia, Brazil and listening to the traditional music of Trinidad and Tobago. And, of course, my favorite is the yoga with the sunrise in Bangkok, Thailand, before the day's first meeting.

I still vividly remember those moments. They made every mission and long hour of work worthwhile and enjoyable. They comforted my perception of myself as an artist, allowing my heart and creativity to guide everything I do. I felt like I was in a movie; every setup had its music and stage. The hard work accompanied it all. That was who I was then—and who I am now. All the reports and deliverables reflected those connections that anchored the beauty of the developmental mission for "a World Free of Poverty." I loved every moment!

As a leader, bringing your work back to the people around you, the connections you create with them, and the service you provide for them is essential.

Several questions for you to find answers to and make sense of your work so that you can unleash the legend and the artist by connecting with your most creative way of being:

> *Who are you doing this for?*
> *Who are you impacting by your decision, by your initiative, and through your project?*
> *Whose life are you changing today?*
> *What inspires your creativity?*

Leadership Requires the Creativity of an Artist

When you lead yourself, you need to find new ways, develop new ideas and take new approaches. This creativity is required even in your strategic context when you revive your strategy repeatedly as the world advances.

You need to be at the top of your field to become a pioneer within your expertise and to show up and evolve each time. It takes innovation and creativity, and they both come with inspiration.

Find out what inspires you most and integrate it into your life. It could be music, nature, art and beauty.

You can also change your taste with time, from classical music to jazz, pop, and opera. You get to choose your mood and where you are. You might prefer art, sculptures and painting. Find your gateway to travel in your mind and escape to a place of creativity and channeling. You will write faster while crafting the most beautiful projects.

Inspiration arises from awakening your senses through smells, sounds, touches, or feelings. To spark your inspiration, integrate these experiences into your daily life. By doing so, you'll enhance your creativity and stimulate innovative ideas. Ultimately, you will be ready to witness musicals and movie scenes unfolding in your own life.

BE THE STAR IN THE MOVIE OF YOUR LIFE

Looking at your life as a movie, every day or every scene will be different. Extracting beauty in every situation: the joyful one, the sad one, the hard one, and the one that needs courage and the one that takes your breath away.

When you look at things that way, you will see harmony in them. The colors match perfectly, and the style somehow goes with the whole decor—that will be in the simplicity of nature and anything in your surroundings.

And the scene is up to you to carry it the way you want to tell it as the most beautiful story of your life. You will start enjoying this way of being as if you were the most attractive character in a movie, from a classical movie with Audrey Hepburn to a James Bond one to a modern life reality. Choose the character that suits you best as the goal achieved and the embodiment of your dream identity. All you need to do then is live by it.

STAND AS AN UNDENIABLE REFERENCE

Focus on establishing yourself as a reference point in your field and area of expertise until you genuinely feel that the legend within you has emerged. Achieving this requires becoming a thought leader and a trusted expert.

Begin by expanding your consciousness to embrace something much greater than the life you were born into, the one modeled for you, or your beliefs. This shift will allow you to step into your desires and fully embrace them. The essence of this Code is about empowerment. Never silence or diminish yourself again.

It takes a lot of courage and empathy toward yourself to do so. Let's play a visualization game together. Stand up and look at yourself in the mirror. As you stare into your eyes, see yourself as the incredible person you want to be—the powerful, joyful, goal-achieved you. Look at your beauty, and be proud of what you see. Look at how relaxed and wise you have become.

Your business is thriving. Your relationships are all in sync with you. Your life is a masterpiece. And you are so proud of every part of you. Look at yourself with your eyes bright and shiny. You are full of confidence and vibrant energy. Hold on to that image. And when you meet her again in the mirror, you tell yourself: "Yes! You did it!"

Smile and keep that beautiful image of yours in your mind. Own it more as you read through these pages.

You are ready to embark on a journey to incredible success and impact when you stand as a leader. That journey will not be easy, but it will be worth every piece until you reach your goals. Finally, your capacity to embrace the duality of life will determine your strength.

Because life will test you and surprise you, your role as a leader of yourself and everything you want to achieve is to accept all the excitement and beauty with grace and gratitude while extracting the lessons and wisdom from everything else.

It takes many ups and downs, successes and failures on the way. Only then will you feel poised to understand how much those lessons are needed to grow more loving and caring. Create your story by accepting your uniqueness and your journey. Build your legacy by showing resilience and seeking excellence in everything you do.

Give the Legend Inside Space to Shine!

Many people need clarification because they continue feeling behind the scenes that they are not enough. They become subject to the imposter syndrome and to the questioning of whether they are deserving of success or not. They start despising the human version of themselves, the one they are at home when no one is looking, the one that enjoys the simple routines of life. Being a mother of four, I learned with time that who you are at home, as a mother, as a daughter, as a sister, is that beautiful human side of you. You should never diminish that part of you to let the legend in you rise.

The greatness of the legend comes from the nourishment of that human part. You should never lose that side—the one that nurtures you with love and care. The simplest things in life bring energy you never knew you had. They ignite your inner spark and light up your fire. People make mistakes as they rise in money and investments, or their level of achievements when they start judging the human in them and drifting away from it—that's when they get lost! The human and the legend will co-exist together forever.

The Legend will rise because of the greatness of the human in you. The legendary version of you is the one that helps you access the spotlight and creates the outlet for you to improve your life and attract abundance and all the luxury you want if you so choose. The human is the one you want to cherish and keep alive.

CASE STUDY FROM THE GLOBAL MASTERMIND COMMUNITY

As a mentor and a business strategist, I have never been more connected and present through the programs I run. We have been celebrating win after win inside our programs for the women. I am so proud of my women clients and the changes they produce when they let their creativity take over. In general, our intuition gets shut off with all the stress, anxiety and overwhelm. Going through the BAL Method sequence and the different codes, they change their life from being puzzled to becoming grounded and organized. Incredible results happen, such as getting promoted and doubling their salaries, launching their project after many years of procrastination, and standing out as empowered leaders and go-to experts. Many success stories are shared every day to inspire other women and to confirm the power of collective intelligence in pushing you and helping calibrate with higher levels of success, love, wealth and recognition, like how Rania celebrated her first million last week after filing for bankruptcy, losing her marriage and everything, in addition to a prolonged depression and gaining so much weight. We did so much healing at the beginning of the 11 months of working together inside the private circle. We started with mindset work and energetics, then set up a strategy and a plan–and she took disciplined and intentional actions. We changed the plan four times that year—but we kept believing, and then she hit her first million. Now, she is on her way to reaching the 8-figure mark.

Business is an art. It requires all your creativity, heart, and an athlete's spirit for flexibility and perseverance. You want to connect first by doing what you love and loving what you do. Then, let the depth of your creativity guide you and trust the artist within you. Only then can you create the space for your legend to rise.

You are both the artist and the masterpiece!

ACTIVITY FOR CODE 8

For these activities, let's tap into our creativity and connect with the legendary artist in us. What type of Art do you feel most connected with?

_____
_____
_____
_____

If you were a legend, what would you be known for? What will you be doing?

_____
_____
_____

If you liberate the Legend in you, what would you see happening in your life?

_____

_____

_____

_____

What would you like to add daily to ignite your senses and nourish your creativity? Choose one or two activities to integrate into your habit.

_____

_____

_____

_____

FINDING THE SPARK

I spent my first year after that lowest point studying and analyzing how the most successful women in the world made it back. I discovered where they get their drive from, their motivation and inspiration, and how they ignite the force within. So many women have done it before us. I wrote the book "African Girl, Africa Woman: How Agile, empowered and Tech-savvy Females Will Transform the Continent... for Good"* in three languages—English, French and Arabic. I dedicate this book to my three girls and every young girl and woman. I needed every example and proof that everything would be okay. I used the words page after page to grow my courage and resilience beyond my limiting beliefs.

The book has the greatest message:

> "To girls,
> do not just lean in; stand up
> Express yourself
> Create
> Study hard

---

* https://www.amazon.com/dp/B092M52XL1

Take your work seriously, but remember how to laugh!

And to women:
You are not alone,
you stand on the shoulders of countless women before you
All who have done and are still accomplishing amazing
     things

They teach, they code, they launch startups,
they finance new ventures, run multinational corpora-
     tions, lead governments
Learn from these role models, from these leaders, and you
     will become one who will inspire the next generation."

I uploaded the book to Amazon first in English and then in French, and every time a copy sold, I was so thrilled. It worked. It happened. Money was coming in, and one book sold after the other. The compound effect was always my favorite part of math. I trusted the channel just opened and was so grateful daily for it. I repeated my mantra, "I am so happy and grateful that money comes to me from multiple sources continuously." A light at the end of a very long and dark tunnel was starting to twinkle, a very small one, but I knew deep inside that no door closes without giving the space for a bigger one to open. The question is when you will notice it.

Then, I started feeling joy and happiness inside me. Even though all the problems were still there, the complications were still there, I felt hope. I felt the happiness within and the peace of mind that started to fill me from inside. Following this moment, the BAL Method came to be. I began selling programs, Masterminds in English and French and private coaching to dive into the business strategy. I reached multiple six figures within a few months. Money is energy–you get to experience it firsthand when you tune into that. It is time for every woman to become living proof of what calibration to the frequency of receiving, succeeding, creating wealth and making an impact means. Read on, my friend!

PART THREE
LEAD

Elevate your Leadership.
Make it a journey to create a Masterpiece out of your life.

We are at the last part of this book, and the leader in you is ready to rise higher than you can ever imagine. Here are four codes to wrap this beautifully while elevating to your greatness.

CODE 9— THE PROSPERITY CODE
CODE 10— THE ENERGETICS OF ABUNDANCE
CODE 11— BE THE ONE
CODE 12— CELEBRATE IN THE NAME OF GRATITUDE

Leadership begins with leading yourself first and then building a lasting legacy.

Your job is to open the receiving channel so you can access all the prosperity the universe has to offer.

To do this, you need to master your connection to energetics and calibrate to the frequency that aligns with your truth and your desires.

As you read through this last part, consider the identity you want to embody: being the ONE.

Be the One who deserves an incredible life.
Be the One destined for greatness.
Be the One meant to turn your dreams into reality.

This mindset allows you to CELEBRATE every step, every achievement, and every level of enlightenment.

Lead yourself to become the most extraordinary human expression of your spiritual perfection!

Create a masterpiece and make a lasting impact while celebrating every step in gratitude for moving forward, no matter how small it may be.

CODE 9
RECEIVING PROSPERITY

A strong mindset is insufficient for a business to thrive without a clear strategy, and why many new entrepreneurs get stuck and many companies fail. You can have the motivation and inspiration but must combine them with a well-structured plan.

Mastering the business plan, cash flows and budgeting, structuring and organization, branding, messaging, and selling process is essential. The book's second part focuses on action-taking. It is about embodying a great leader for your business and your expertise.

Leadership is the integration of it all: strategy, mindset, and energetics—and becoming the best in what you do. It takes knowledge, expertise, and strategy. Your job is to focus on giving the best value and keeping a great mindset. And all the rest will come your way!

I used to sit gazing outside, lost in my thoughts, floating somewhere. I traveled within my mind through what didn't feel right in the past, what didn't work, why it didn't work, what I could have done wrong and why it happened as it did. I thought this was what high-level, super-busy professionals do. They stay occupied in their mind, with an overwhelming feeling of being busy and looking super important!

That way of being didn't work anymore because I was continuously in a vortex of fear and worry. As I deepened my understanding and started teaching about mindset and energetics, I started sensing a growing light of peace and inner joy. When I gazed outside, it felt like a beautiful silence. I didn't know calmness was possible for hard workers, overachievers and leaders—a state of happiness in just being, breathing, and sensing.

The purpose of the head and heart is for you to fill them with gratitude and appreciation for life. The business, the planning, and the money are not to be parked there. Let gratitude and appreciation be that flow of motion, like a passing wave that transcends your body and fuels your inner power.

You surrender by trusting that the waves will carry you to shore and that everything will unfold to bring you beautiful rewards. A game of trust and surrender to a sacred force than all of us!

THE RECEIVING CHANNEL

Prosperity is the state of being prosperous and feeling abundant. Abundance refers to different aspects of our lives—money, love, relationships, and respect. Some things happen through our actions, while others happen by letting the universe take care of them. Receiving money, prosperity, and wealth is in the realm of energetics.

Being receptive and staying in the receiving mode is something you want to become accustomed to, so much so that as I write this, I feel like upgrading our Mantra now to say, "I receive love, respect and magic money." Attracting and manifesting is one part of the story. But the shift you need to see happening in your life is about becoming the receiving channel. That very door you want to keep wide open without letting any feeling of guilt, shame or "why-me?" get into you.

We live in a dualistic world where there is both feminine energy and masculine energy. The Feminine energy is about trust, knowing deep inside your connection with the universe, where everything happens with your being. Masculine energy focuses on doing and taking action. It is the toolbox we spend our lives filling with knowledge and experience. We have both of them inside–women and men. Our task is to learn how to navigate through those energies so we can move with the flow. The wrong tool can be frustrating and ruin what should be yours to receive.

The objective of this code is to unlock the receiving sequence. While taking action is about doing, and believing is about being. This part is about 'having,' which means the energy experience is entirely different from the human experience. This distinction calls for more clarity in the tools used and a distinction between what works in the human realm and what is ruled by energetics. Using the wrong tools will halt your aspirations and path to reaching your goals. Thus, when you pray and meditate a lot, but nothing is happening, you need to start taking action. If you overwork yourself, drain yourself, and try everything but still do not receive the desired results, this shows the need to let more feminine energy into your life and your way of being. Receiving is in the realm of feminine power. Let's start with the frequency of money.

Money is Energy—Let it Flow

Let's turn to money because one of the most eye-opening insights I gained is that money is an energetic currency. It flows when you let it, and it goes where people are happy to receive it and spend it.

So why does it seem so hard for us to receive money?

It feels hard because it often seems like a pressure too heavy to carry. Indeed, it links tightly to feelings of unworthiness and not feeling at ease with receiving gifts or being invited to restaurants. Receiving can sometimes trigger a sensation of guilt, shame, or even blame for not being able to return the same, do the same. All of those confusing feelings put a block on the receiving thread. The receiving frequency is tied to gratitude, love, joy, and abundance, while all the shame, guilt, and fear link to lack. We tend to perpetuate the feelings where we park ourselves. To attract money into our lives, we must master the energetics behind it.

Our subconscious mind has a paradigm that works like software with sophisticated programming. Emotional codes connected to people, relationships, money, and everything else constituting our human experience make up that programming. These small codes or unprocessed emotions bring negativity because they connect with old beliefs and events. They get triggered when something reminds us of them. Just like one line from a movie or a song, it will bring so many memories of how we used to feel when we heard it. We may even recreate the exact scene of the movie as if we were watching it again.

When it comes to money, we often link it to worry. Will it be enough to finish the month? Will I get paid on time? Will I make enough money to buy a house, get a new car, maintain the garden, and enroll my children in the best schools? The list goes on and on. We attach so much fear to money that the emotional coding of anxiety and worry from lack becomes linked to money-related thoughts.

Now, if our subconscious mind is all made of emotional coding, the moment they get triggered, we need to honor them and let them pass by processing them instead of hating and ignoring or trying to fix them by working harder and trying more. That will use masculine energy to fix a feminine issue—which does not work by conception. What happens when we try to resolve the situation? We freeze the energy and all the emotions that come with it. At the same time, every emotion naturally keeps the energy flowing perpetually. That is the normal state.

Throughout our lives, we experience a wide range of emotions that can cause us to freeze when we attempt to suppress discomfort and annoyance. Regardless of what they are, processing these feelings invites us to honor and allow them to flow. You have the power to rewire yourself and create a new identity.

Usually, we wonder what to do when we don't feel good and have feelings that make us uncomfortable. In that situation, you only have to let feelings pass. This is why emotional intelligence is so important to master. It helps you navigate with all the feminine energy you have inside. When creating new coding, you build your knowledge regarding what to expect, who you are, and what to do. And this is key when it comes to manifestation.

MANIFESTATION NEEDS ALIGNMENT

Manifestation does not rely on what you think; it works with what you genuinely believe and know deep inside. You must surrender and allow yourself to feel your emotions until the old beliefs crumble, which enables you to create the new beliefs you want to align with. Only then will you be ready to manifest. Ultimately, we attract what aligns with us, reflecting our inner dialogue and the narrative within our emotional minds.

Manifestation connects with the quantum field of energetics. To access this field of energetics, you must learn how to sit with your feelings. It is okay to feel bad because something does not or might not work. Know that you can honor the feeling until it passes by, knowing deep inside that you will be alright no matter what.

We often stop believing or changing our wiring because we avoid everything that makes us feel inadequate and uncomfortable. To feel safe, we think about how things will not work anyway and keep ourselves in the "comfortable" zone that we have created and made comfortable simply from habits. This is why many people find themselves locked in underpaid responsibilities or a 9-to-5 job they do not appreciate.

Each one of us is born worthy, and nothing has changed. Even though experiences and circumstances complicate things, your worth of love, respect, and money will never change. It will always be there. We know that we are a spiritual creation in a human body that can tap into the limitless abundance of the universe. So what could hold us back? When you are not tapping into this limitless abundance, it is always because you are avoiding feeling bad.

All you need is to be unshakably convinced that you will be okay no matter what.

You boost your confidence through reassuring and recurrent results or by winging it that you will be okay even if you don't receive what you want, even if you fail or lose. Repeat this: believe in it, know it deep inside.

When you dwell on what feels wrong and uncomfortable, you become aligned with it and attract more of it. But when you let the feelings pass while sitting disconnected from them, you create a new wiring, a new coding, and a new knowing. Then, your whole experience with alignment shifts to the side you want. I call this conscious awareness, which helps you do whatever you desire.

You will crack the code once you understand how your energetics should mirror a trend of consistent elevation. It comes with your growth and development throughout your life. Starting with sadness is okay as long as you are true to yourself. Evolution means a continuous change–emotions will always pass if you honor them and let them be processed. Nothing is stagnant, and we are the reflection of all those emotions inside us.

TIME SHOULD BE YOUR ALLY

One significant shift you need to make is about time. Time should become your ally, even though this is not always true. There are a few sentences we keep repeating mechanically out of habit, such as: "I don't have time to do this or to do that," "If only I had more time," and "I need more time for this and that."

When you wire your thoughts around the lack of time., the first thing that comes to mind is to learn how to manage time. Different tools and tables help organize time, routines, and a time management scheme to make you feel on top of your time. But all of this would not help if you don't understand how time is your ally. When you start rushing and stressing about the lack of time, you lose calmness and control over yourself and will not get any of it back. And as you get too emotional about time, you become frustrated.

If our connection with time comes from a space of lack due to the continuous complaints about the lack of–time, this will create more of that energy around you.

We wire ourselves by creating patterns and replicating them in various aspects of our lives. This is why how we approach one task often determines how we approach everything else.

The feeling you want to entertain is that things are happening on their time and that everything will be okay, which gives you a sense of calmness and abundance, which creates prosperity. The opposite is fear, guilt, shame, and worry. And those are the feelings of people who are not convinced or conscious that they will have money.

By drawing a parallel, we see that a lack of money consistently links to a lack of time. It is clear that healing your relationship with time should come before working on your relationship with money.

We can always use time more effectively. We will never feel lacking if we recognize that everything we need is already within us. This understanding eliminates any reason to feel a sense of scarcity and encourages us to embrace abundance.

When we understand how everything exists in the realm of energetics, if we could only see them, we would realize we can have everything we want. But the reality is that we don't see them. Do we need the patience to see it through? When we want things done, we want them now and fast. Impatience and wanting everything now and fast—of this speedy digital era makes time look scarce when it lasts more than the window allocated in our illusionary vision. What we need to change is not the amount of time it takes. One more day, one more month, or even one more year before achieving our goal will not change it. What matters is the timing. It is the alignment of what you want and how the universe and every external thing synchronize jointly to bring it to fruition.

Thus, speed–to gain time–is not the answer to prosperity and achieving your goals. What matters is intentionality. The question you should ask yourself is: what can I accomplish in the space of time that I have?

When you dwell in the field of lack—lack of time, lack of money, lack of opportunity, you will attract more of it, so says the Law of Attraction. You attract the field you dwell in as you become aligned with it.

Become Intentional With Time

By understanding that time is on your side, you start using it to create an extraordinary life and trust the timing of things as they happen. Your goals are inevitable when you believe in them and remain focused on them while taking action.

Become intentional about everything you do and understand that you can operate in multiple dimensions in time. Every action you take, and everything you say is good for the moment you do it—and also for later. If you write a book, an article, or a post, it is read the moment you write it and will continue to impact as more and more people find it and read it.

Intentionality applies to anything you do or say, particularly in an argument. Ask yourself if it is suitable for now and if it will be ideal later. When you become aware of this intertwining reality between now and later, you start living in multiple dimensions of time. Every good you do will multiply with time. Every action you take will have an impact on different timelines. When they align, you quantum leap to another space, collapsing time and wrapping it on itself.

It does not matter how long it takes for someone to come in as a client, for a contract to be signed, or for any opportunity to show up at your doorstep; the timing matters. All of what we want to achieve, the objectives, and the relationships are co-creations between you and others. This co-creation happens when the timing is suitable for all the involved parties. **And timing is not something you do. It is something you trust in**.

We need not care how fast we get to our objective. What matters is that we do get there. When we plant a seed, it takes time to grow it. Some seeds may take three months, others nine for human gestation, and up to 18 to 22 months for elephants. Similarly, flowers and trees vary from one month for bushes to 18 months for pineapples. You can do nothing when the seeds are in the ground; water them and trust the process. Giving it love will help you calibrate to its vibration and make the journey enjoyable. If every action we take is a seed we plant, we must provide it with time, watering it with care and love before it manifests. Until one day, you will plant and harvest seeds you have planted and trusted to grow with time. Holding the vision without any evidence of it happening means embracing the void, the emptiness, and the space where nothing exists yet. This state reassures you that you are moving in the right direction. You must surrender to the process and allow it to take the time it needs to unfold.

CASE STUDY FROM THE GLOBAL MASTERMIND COMMUNITY

In this very spirit, when Leyla joined our French program, the Club of Femme Leaders Experience, she was a senior flight attendant with over 20 years of experience. Her dream was to become a manager, allocate programs to different flight crews, and do all the monitoring and coordination that comes with it. The airline company had never promoted a non-engineering person to that job. We worked on her alignment with the job and her readiness to lead, and after six months into the program, we all marveled at how she landed that job and became the first flight attendant ever to hold a managerial position. Leyla is proof of the power of readiness to receive and lead herself through all the limiting beliefs and constraints of what had become the norm.

I am so proud of all the incredible women inside our community and their success stories and amazing transformations.

THE SUCCESS TRIAD REFLECTS THE PRISM OF PROSPERITY

Success has different meanings for each person. It can range from reaching significant achievements and attracting wealth to creating a quiet and peaceful life.

But what we all have in common is that we agree that success is a journey and not a destination. We thrive on our objectives and goals. But as soon as we get closer to one of them, new ones appear on the horizon. It becomes an everlasting endeavor.

There are also cases where we might give up before getting closer to what we want to hold in our hands and manifest in our lives. And we add to that many questions: Why do we do so? Is it from a lack of motivation or inspiration? Or is it more concerning our inner power and capacity to stay resilient and focused no matter what?

These past few years, I have been studying what makes people successful. I discovered that lasting success is beyond the old paradigm of getting the best degrees, the best first job, and setting up the top strategy. It takes more than that. There are two more dimensions that you need to master for you to create the prism of success, wealth, and recognition. I refer to this as the Success Triad: (1) a solid foundation of expertise, strategy, and planning, (2) an unshakable mindset and a focused attitude, and (3) a third one about energetics and alignment to a solid inner force.

Let's review these concepts now to integrate them fully. With all the contemplation we did together in this book, you should feel more advanced in them by now.

Strategy and Planning

Setting up the right strategy is essential. It gives you a solid foundation to stand on. The more sound and solid the plan is, the more it can be translated into a thorough implementation scheme that will bring inevitable success.

You want to achieve excellence in everything you do because it will always make you stand out. Most importantly, you want a strategic plan to keep growing and set up a system to support your vision. Excellence means acquiring all the knowledge and doing the work repeatedly until you become the best version of yourself for your expertise, the service you provide, or the product you create.

When it comes to planning, it calls for discipline and continuity. Often, when a plan doesn't work, it is not because it was wrong. No, it was simply never finished. Finally, for planning to succeed, it should integrate every part of what you need to reinforce, from being business-savvy and tech-savvy to mastering your branding, communication, leadership, and being the boss of your work and professional career.

Building a powerful Mindset

Leading yourself to success requires so much courage. And that courage is needed when fear kicks in. We will undoubtedly encounter fear if we aspire to create significant objectives and dreams. As an entrepreneur or as a high-level executive, some moves might feel bold and scary. Then you can either let them overwhelm you and wait for the fear to settle down or swallow the fear and grab the courage simultaneously to overcome it and move through it. This is when the mindset starts playing the vital role it is supposed to have.

Our mind is structured so that only 5% is intellectual and conscious, and the rest—95%—is the unconscious and emotional mind. Strategy and reasoning represent only 5%, while the rest is a cumulation of programming and old beliefs and habits from the past. Creating a powerful mindset means using your mind to bring yourself closer to your results.

Understanding your mind possesses the power of focus, which you will bring into your life whatever you focus on. It is time to stop focusing on everything that makes you worry and scared about the invisible future. Shifting your mindset is about having a positive attitude. Things will always work out with perseverance and consistency. And the right attitude will make the impossible possible and help you create wealth and recognition. A positive mindset will strengthen your inner power and help you attract the right circumstances and conditions, getting you closer to your dream objective.

Aligning with the Energetics

The third dimension of the success triad is the most powerful and intriguing one. Taking it from a scientific perspective helps you elevate to new heights using logical reasoning. It connects to your emotional intelligence and the way you feel inside. When we talk about energetics, we talk about frequency and vibrations. The subject is fascinating as it brings me back to my days at Harvard, inside the Physics department and the courses in Quantum Physics. Back in the mid-nineties, it was all above my head and intriguing. How can we use these concepts in real life? Let's start by understanding that vibrations mirror our internal emotions.

Thus, when we are in a vortex of worry, fear, doubt, rage, shame, and other negative emotions, we attract more of them. Thus, they rank very low in the Hertz cone of frequencies. While the frequency of joy brings joy, the frequency of abundance brings abundance. Those high frequencies of love and happiness are also those of money and prosperity.

To attract what you want in life, it is essential to align with the frequency of that desire. That match must represent the truth, which can be challenging since the truth always resonates at the highest frequency. We often need help to believe in receiving what we cannot yet see. Therefore, creating an energetic projection to ensure accurate alignment is a crucial first step. The most effortless alignment you can embody will reflect an energetic projection of improvement and growth.

Finally, the success triad is about bringing light into your life. It is a way to create your prism of prosperity and abundance, attract incredible wealth, make a lasting impact, and achieve the extraordinary. The most important thing is to be able to navigate through the journey with grace and confidence. The structure of the triad would ensure that you build a solid foundation of strategy and a clear action plan, a strong mindset, and focused thinking. At the same time, you stand behind an energetic projection of continuous improvement and development.

1 2 3... let's become receptive to all the prosperity the universe has to offer.

ACTIVITY FOR CODE 9

To open the channel of prosperity, you must be receptive and fully aligned with the receiving frequency—love, joy, abundance, money, and prosperity.

The activity for this code is to rewire your subconscious mind to align with the thread of love, joy, wealth, and prosperity. This is a mantra for you to rewire your paradigm and use it as your truth.

> *"I attract Love, Respect and Magic Money always, always.*
> *"I receive Love, Respect and Magic Money always, always."*

Write it down and repeat it over and over again:

_____

_____

_____

_____

WE ARE IN A CO-CREATION WITH THE UNIVERSE

Growing up, we spent our vacations visiting family on my mother's side in Tunisia. We did this repeatedly until I was nineteen and went to study in Paris, at which point I let that habit slip away. Although we returned for a family reunion much later, many years passed, yet the memories remained. I recall long nights spent gazing at the stars, swimming in the warm, inviting waters of Chebba on Tunisia's southern Mediterranean coast, across from Italy. The water was warm, transparent, and delightful. I fondly remember windsurfing, boating, swimming, and collecting crabs from the rocks.

We had the most beautiful, exciting, romantic and fun summers any teenager could imagine. We laughed, danced, played, felt love and romance, dreamed of an exciting life, hoped for the most beautiful future and did it all together with the innocence and naivety of youth.

After thirty years, I returned to my childhood summer house as I write this. I took my children to get some of the vibes their Mum enjoyed at their age. The first evening, they lay down on the floor in the house with the open ceiling, looking at the stars. I told them this was where I dreamed of going to Harvard and reaching the highest decision-making spheres. It felt like I went back to my starting point.

I was overwhelmed with emotion. I wanted to write this book, but the feelings were too strong to ground myself and sit down to do it. I wanted to feel everything. The emotional memories I thought were so real. We keep everything somewhere in the subconscious mind, and we forget about them. I had a calling to go back to that land where my grandmother was from, the one that encouraged me and inspired me, and the one I keep in my heart and in everything I do. I went back, looking for a clue. The clue came with unwrapping these codes, finding new paths I could have never imagined possible. What if there was a possibility of a quantum leap to another level?

Opportunities appeared in my life out of nowhere. They made me believe again in miracles and a power greater than all of us. We are closing multi-million dollar deals as I find my path back to my childhood source of light!

I followed my heart and am so excited about what is coming next. While navigating the field of potentialities, I have unveiled something precious. I surrendered to it with all the grace, feminine energy, and pure love.

Listen to your heart and embrace the most straightforward aspects of being human as you develop your inner legend. You'll discover yourself in the realm of miracles and endless possibilities, where the essence of aligning with the extraordinary resides. Let's explore this concept further within this code.

CODE 10
The Energetics of Abundance

Year after year, I recreated myself over and over. When I look at it today, in hindsight, it kept my passion alive and gave me stamina and the thrill of a forever new starter. I sometimes wonder how I could do it when it gets too hard.

The more I deepened my work around personal and inner development, the more I started seeing the patterns of needing to restart each time. Yes, you can recreate yourself because it is part of the growth. But you should not change because you only know how to climb the slope and overcome the impossible.

As I became more intentional about every move, I started understanding that elevation can happen without starting all over each time. Elevation defines an up-leveling in the frequency with which you vibrate energetically. Simply, it means the type of emotions you feel and the state of mind you dwell in until they become your truth.

This code is for you to master the connection with energetics and to understand how to align with the frequency of love, joy, peace of mind and abundance.

The shift starts when you understand and touch the appreciation of where you are and become intentional about your elevation to a higher level. It does not mean starting all over but more a recalibration to the purity of energetics and the rewiring of your inner coding.

In your own human experience of life and the challenges that come with it, elevation means extracting the lessons and the wisdom. Elevation will make you feel grown and strengthened to move to another level, where it can only get better than where you were before.

The moment you start seeing it as an elevation, your mindset will shift. In hindsight, you will become an energetic match to the frequency of ongoing growth and evolution of life.

You should reflect this way of being in your business, brand, personal life, and all your connections–parents, friends, collaborators, team members, and everyone else.

Finally, Leadership requires excellence, a powerful mindset, and an energetic projection of love, innovation and development. It is all about the projection of energies.

ENERGETICS AND EMOTIONS

Emotional intelligence and understanding energetics are similar to cracking new codes in your life. People around you can download it from you and calibrate it for them. It connects with your light so that you can shine through it.

Strength and perseverance are essential for success but do not stem solely from strategic planning and hard work. Your emotional state and mindset closely influence the essence of success. We often hear and emphasize that success is not about doing different things; it's about doing things differently, and different means a different emotional state —experiencing emotions that are more nurturing, encouraging, and aligned with the force of life. This is what emotional intelligence is about.

Therefore, to deepen your understanding of emotional intelligence, it is essential to distinguish between the different powers you have in your hands to navigate through the various facets of life—both professional and personal. On one hand, circumstantial power comes from the outside world; on the other hand, inner power unlocks from within.

The more emotional intelligence leaders master, the more they will stand out and achieve success. Leaders become leaders through their ability to influence other people's thinking, emotions, and actions—the starting point for that is affecting their emotions!

Examples from the Global Mastermind Community

Our programs focus on calibrating feelings related to success, excellence, a shining brand, wealth creation, and making an impact. This approach helps us celebrate incredible wins within the Leaders Mastermind. A new level of leadership, such as new board member positions, winning an election, and getting a new promotion for Anna and Rania. A new level of wealth, like going from 10,000 USD per month to 10,000 USD per week to 10,000 USD per day for Sonia as an executive coach. A redefined mission to broaden the context and create a deep alignment of thoughts, emotions, and actions. A new book or three new books, instead. New international awards for Amira and Vanessa, recognitions and a standing ovation after a big speech for Kenza and Sam in our private VIP circle!

I created the BAL Method* to encompass various programs to help you find guidance by tapping into your genius and standing out as a great leader. This mentorship focuses on developing a perfectly tailored strategy for you to win and prosper. My objective with this material is to empower everyone to build the courage to explore possibilities and potentialities, embracing the mindset of "what if the extraordinary happens" until you create that extraordinary around you. This approach enables you to lead yourself to wealth and impact while fully embracing every part of yourself.

Go Beyond Circumstantial Power

The circumstantial power comes from the education you could get, the job, the respected position, the family that supports you while growing

---

* www.balmethod.com

up, and the backing you get from outside conditions and realities. It is all drawn from circumstances.

That circumstantial power helps you grow more confident and independent. It also gives you a sense of reassurance when needed. Thus, when following an expected path for career development, that power will guide you to getting promoted as a manager and holding a leadership position.

However, the reality is more complex. On your journey, many events could alter your path, shaking your confidence and putting you off track. There are also moments when circumstances can become a burden. Not having the strength to carry the weight of all the expectations society and family have placed on your shoulders will deepen your lack of self-worth.

That is when you can no longer rely on the circumstantial power you have been so used to leaning on. You need resilience, which connects directly to your inner power. I experienced this firsthand when faced with significant corporate challenges and watched all the circumstantial power crumble in front of my eyes. There was nothing I could rely on anymore, not even a loving arm that would hold me without letting some of "I told you," "I knew it," and "how could you" slip in what was supposed to be a comforting voice. I still tear up thinking or writing about those moments. I don't think I will ever heal completely from it, but I know that I tattooed on my heart a lifetime reminder of all the lessons and wisdom I could extract from it. A friend, an international corporate lawyer, looked at me in one of those tough meetings and told me, "When you play in the financial sphere, it is like sitting at the table to play poker. So the moment you sit, that's the moment you undeniably agreed to play."

You will never know what cards you will get when rolling the dice. The game is on, and you need to abide by its rules. The more you understand the energetics, the more you will grasp your capacity to influence the dice results by concentrating on the dice flipping in the air. Sending it positivity instead of expecting the worst so that you feel you are right —and you can enjoy the few minutes of feeling safe from being right.

In a poker game, there are winners and losers, and you need to own the outcomes–precisely the way they are because they are what they are.

I studied this concept repeatedly, contemplating what it meant in our lives.

When circumstances are not in your favor, don't dwell on them. There is nothing you can do about them! Just move on and accept them as they are. Michael Beckwith[*] explains it as a sign from the universe forcing you to change direction. Either way, you need to tap into the reservoir of power from within—this is inner power.

SWITCH TO INNER POWER

By unlocking your inner power, you will see it grow strong and override your circumstantial power. The best analogy to describe Inner Power is a backup generator. For electricity, all the houses rely on the city's electrical network. Electricity is supplied daily through the network and feels fluid, easy and normal. Until one day, when electricity stops because of a problem in the network or a shortage, what happens then? Can a house keep running with no electricity? Impossible. Everything in the fridge would spoil. There is no way any house could live without electricity today for an extended period. Many homes have individual generators installed that automatically kick on when electricity from the network is no longer available so they can avoid the results of outages.

Inner power is similar to a backup generator. It is a source within that does not need installation because it is already there, waiting for you to tap into it.

The source comes from within and feeds from your strong belief in your worth and path toward growth and evolution. Your inner power will help you create the circumstances you long for when you don't find them. You use it to stand confident and empowered if you become defeated by circumstantial power. You unleash your inner power as you crack the codes of your emotional intelligence.

This code is about understanding energetics and how you can align them with who you are and want to be. Energetics are about your feelings and your connection with them.

---

[*] https://www.amazon.com/Life-Visioning-Transformative-Activating-Potential/dp/1622030508

What makes a difference among leaders and what distinguishes empowered and great leaders is their emotional intelligence. They are aware of their feelings, and mastering their emotions allows their intelligence to remain unshakable no matter what. When your feelings are strained day after day, they will impact your performance. Furthermore, they will affect your decision-making process. On average, we make around three thousand decisions a day. Some are important, and some are as simple as what side to start brushing your teeth. Either way, becoming emotionally shaken affects us and alters our reasoning, logic, and thinking processes. Therefore, making decisions will be impacted directly.

> *We want to have absolute power. That means no matter what.*
> *No matter what, you will overcome the struggle you experience.*
> *No matter what, you will learn how to be an energetic match for wealth.*
> *No matter what, you will create an extraordinary life.*
> *No matter what, you will do it with grace and beauty.*

Leading yourself to greatness means mastering every rule and every move, just like in any game. When circumstances aren't favorable, you unleash your inner power. Cracking this code is understanding that the whole game of self-leadership starts with your inner power. It is not about how hard you work but how strong and long you can keep at it.

Don't wait for life to come to you; take charge and reclaim your power. You need to pursue it yourself. The Believe Act Lead Method is so powerful. It is for you to accelerate the process, master your emotional intelligence, define the best-fit strategy and go for it, create a global brand, and build your legacy. It works inside our programs with the understanding of the process, integrating all those codes with discipline and intentionality. You can turn your life around and attract wealth, love and opportunities beyond your dreams!

Find the Courage to Lead

Tapping into your inner power is the start of a rebirth or an elevation beyond anything you could expect. It means using a parallel dimension that you cannot touch or see. We can only feel and trust its existence. This is where faith becomes essential, your connection with spirituality and the more prominent force.

What do you do when things get hard, and circumstances are no longer there to hold you? Do you just stop being who you are and who you aspire to become? No, don't you stop! Remember that you still have so much you haven't seen. So much you haven't done.

Why would you stop now? Why would you let the lack of circumstances stop you? Why would you let the illusion of inexistent hope bury you? Why wouldn't you give yourself the right to believe in a better future?

As you read, you might think: because it is too much, too heavy, and too difficult to apprehend. But in the field of potentiality and miracles, there is another dimension—light and energy. It can never be blocked or held anywhere. It flows. It rises. It always finds a way. Like water, it will always find ways to slip through the cracks and create a little passage.

Your resilience and courage will make a difference in your success.

Resilience comes from your emotional strength and belief that you will reach your goals and persevere no matter what. It comes from a power deeply anchored in you, a power fueled by trusting its very existence. When you genuinely believe in it being there for you, you will calibrate to it and start feeling the force of life. There is a fine line between spirituality and the universe's infinite power. The more you feel connected to it, the more you notice resilience growing.

Resilience calls for courage. And when there is fear, you need courage. Courage would not be required if there was no fear. Courage is the fuel to a better life, a rebirth, and to any elevation. You don't need to dig deep inside to look for courage. It doesn't come from within. Courage comes from outside, from a profound inspiration. Courage has an external source. It comes from knowing that you will be okay no matter what.

I found my courage when I needed it more by looking at my three daughters and remembering how much hope they have in me, their mum, their role model, and their strength. What have they got to do with my corporate difficulties—nothing. They have not asked for it and should not be affected by it. There is no room for any collateral damage. I still recall the day I promised myself that I would always be there to protect them, no matter what. It's a promise I want to keep so they can hold on to their beautiful and innocent optimism—like children, full of life and possibilities, bubbling with dreams and excitement about life, about what's for dinner or the next vacation. I couldn't take that away from them!

With that courage, I swallowed all my fear and knew how hard it would be to work through the deluge inside my subconscious mind. What helped me was my deep dive into understanding human behavior and how to change old paradigms. I got mentored, coached and received psychological help–I couldn't take the voyage inside my emotions and my mind on my own in the beginning. Then, I graduated from it all. However, as a leader, you remain a student of leadership forever.

Courage is knowing your emotions and not letting them override everything else. Courage equates to your level of emotional intelligence and maturity. Unleashing the life force and getting the courage to try again and again to preserve and turn your vision into reality is tightly linked to your level of maturity when it comes to understanding your emotions. They feed into each other. Courage boosts your emotional intelligence, and emotional intelligence enhances your courage. It radiates, inspiring others and helping you create your success story.

EMOTIONAL MATURITY

Emotional maturity is related to your readiness to manage and control your emotions. The more you can influence your feelings and those of others, the more you will stand out as a true leader in your field of expertise.

Emotional maturity is the catalyst for your inner power and the force that enables you to create opportunities when none exist. Your level of emotional mastery determines your ability to achieve your goals and create remarkable success in your life. This connection between emotional intelligence and leadership makes great leaders stand out!

The more you understand energetics, the more you see how they intertwine with your emotional intelligence. Applying them in your life starts with comprehending the balance between feminine and masculine energies and knowing when to use each one.

In the masculine paradigm, everything is about results, strategies, systems and executing action plans. We all grew up in this paradigm, which is about achievements, studying hard, getting the best results, preparing for interviews, landing the right job, and working harder and harder. It is, therefore, all about doing and, when finished, doing it all over again.

In the world of energetics, we navigate by embracing all of our feminine energy. Because feminine energy is the incarnation of feelings and being who you are.

When you take a moment to contemplate your life, you will realize that everything revolves around feelings. The more we feel, the more we remember. The more we feel, the more we create connections around the world.

If I ask you today as you read this, would you remember what you had for lunch the same day last week, or would you probably need to stop for a moment to think before being able to respond? A random day is tough to recall unless it was a romantic lunch, a high-powered lunch full of excitement and expectations–or something emotionally distressing. We don't remember what we do unless we anchor it in an emotional memory. To make it emotional, we need to surround the experience with feelings—whether good or bad. It's the feelings that help us remember the moment. They bring us back to the present, creating an emotional memory and making it easier to recall.

Emotions are our memories and all the coding we have accumulated and carefully placed in our subconscious mind. The latter becomes stacked with emotions and feelings triggered by our five sensors–the smell, the touch, the hearing, the eyesight and the taste—through anything that will remind us of a situation.

All you want is to navigate the pressure and everything around you. It is essential to be on top of your emotions—not to stop them but to process them by letting them pass and feeling them through, just like watching part of a movie.

We have become accustomed to working hard and absorbing all the knowledge, using the same tools in every facet of our lives, including energetics. However, this only works once you understand that success is more than that. Bringing the feminine energy opens your perspectives to a whole new dimension.

The more you understand how to connect with it, the more you rewire your mind to receive and honor the divinity within (Code 4-The Force of Life). By grounding your emotions, you raise your vibration. When you align with the frequency of what you want to bring into your life, you become a magnet to your desire, not by doing but by attracting what you want.

EVOLUTION AND GROWTH

The process is a journey of growth and self-development. Every day, we learn new things. Everything we feel becomes heightened and compounded to more.

There might be days where nothing happens, no change, no advancement. But as long as the overall trend is one of ascension, even if we stagnate or go backward at times, it is just to anchor more of the wisdom we need to step up to the next phase. How much contemplation and zooming out do we need to reach significant results?

You need the embodiment of a lifelong journey of evolution, betterment, growth, and elevation. The way we operate, we want things always to be good. It shows up as soon as you finish a task, a project, a presentation, an exam, a meeting, a conference or something similar; you don't like it as much anymore. You become a perfectionist. You only spot what is missing or what could be improved.

At first, you might think it is perfectionism or self-sabotaging—but in reality, it is far from both. You simply have matured and grown after that very experience. At that moment, what you did before feels below your new level of maturity and added knowledge. Instead of beating yourself up or dismissing who you were or what you have achieved, fill your heart with gratitude for your growth, betterment, and evolution. Tomorrow, you will be a better version of yourself—wiser and more experienced, with new knowledge and lessons, whether easy or difficult. Adopting this attitude is what will help you reach your goal. How can you be the best of yourself today, better than yesterday? You want to wear a growth trend and calibrate to it with all your thinking, mindset and energetics.

While it is essential to love what you do and do what you love, it is okay if you aren't there yet. It does not define who you are. It is your path to becoming who you want to be while doing what you love. Bless what you are doing, and feel love and gratitude for the opportunity to have it.

Stay focused on what you love to do and work on becoming great at it. Continuously taking these actions will allow you to align with your goals until you finally achieve them.

THE BEAUTY OF LIFE COMES FROM YOUR OWN EYES

Change the glasses through which you see your life. Create a new filter, and trust the shift of the energetics to help you. In Code 5, we saw how to turn the context into a lens for the year. Now, let's make that lens more positive. As you navigate your day, focus only on the good and ignore everything else. This approach requires discipline and intentionality in finding and focusing on the positive aspects. All the rest will slip away with time. You will begin to see only the good and appreciate how good life is.

There is a reason we are born when we are. Nothing happens haphazardly. Everything is interconnected and synchronized. The more you believe in it, the more you see proof of it unfolding in front of your eyes. Your footprint, astrological identity, and emotional pattern define your existence. Our role is to make our lives the best representation of our being and who we are.

Embody this today and aim to become the best version of yourself, aligning with evolution and seeking personal growth and wisdom. Your mission should focus on giving your best in everything you offer and every task you do so that you transfer your understanding and ensure it lands where it is supposed to be.

Finally, we want to make our very existence the best expression of who we are. Reflecting all these universal realities, the seen and the unseen.

ACTIVITY FOR CODE 10

Sit and journal with this message.

Grab your courage, stamina, resilience, and all the love in your heart. Stand tall no matter what. When you feel scrambled, overwhelmed, or swamped, get the courage from around you. Surround yourself with loved ones or a caring mentor—whatever makes you think you will be okay.

Courage after courage will build momentum, your wisdom will deepen, and you will grow so brave that you will rise higher than ever.

When you reconnect with yourself, you can draw joy from within and surrender to the universal intelligence, the divine, or the power of nature. This process cultivates resilience and nurtures the love within you.

Gratitude will take over and will help you recreate a new paradigm inside you. No matter what you go through, there is no reason not to stand tall. During the most challenging moments, you need to have the best attitude!

The key is in your hand; use it to open the channel for abundance, love, joy and success!

With this new shift, what will be your move going forward?

_____
_____
_____
_____
_____
_____
_____
_____
_____
_____
_____
_____
_____
_____
_____
_____

RISE LIKE A PHOENIX

When I found myself in the red zone of negative millions of dollars somewhere in my entrepreneurial journey, I panicked, lost sleep, lost taste of everything. I was down in a very negative vortex. I went through all those Codes individually to make it back as an average person. I kept my scientific hat to understand them genuinely surrender to self-development and the spiritual dimension that held the light we all seek.

One sentence I heard and integrated is how you could lose everything, but no one could take away your intelligence. This sentence kept repeating itself, but I didn't know how to use it for anything.

What do you do when you feel marginalized, unwelcome, and pointed at with all the fingers? As if that weren't enough, stories and dramas create, transform, and shape around your failure. How do you keep your sanity?

A strong will and a promise to myself kept me going—holding on to the power of one. One action at a time will help you recreate yourself. It does not have to be significant. It just needs to be consistent. It will compound on itself. I knew my story would help many in their lives and through their struggles. I knew that all the wisdom I could not see nor grasp through those very tough moments would be so powerful and propel anyone to levels higher than you could conceive. The sky is not the limit anymore.

Of course, doubt will creep in at times, but you learn within the codes to dust it off and regain your focus. This exact moment is when you need discipline—and understanding that everything has its timing. You will be okay no matter what.

If you want success, there is only one rule: you simply cannot quit!

You are the only ONE to make it work and to rise like a Phoenix!

The energy changes if you do the work without believing in yourself and what you do. Success is not about doing different things; success is about doing what you do with a different mindset. You want to be wrapped in positive energy and aligned with the energetic thread of love, joy, hope and gratitude—the same as abundance and prosperity.

The big question is how we do it.

That question will remain until it changes to another one–and that will be: How did I do it? We embark on our journey with all our leadership and fill our hearts with a readiness to receive all we can magnetize on the way. Nothing happens with a magical wand—like how my 6-year-old just started to understand how the magical wand she bought at Disneyland is not real. This whole process will still be magical. The moment you reach your dream goal, the journey will feel enchanted.

CODE 11

BEING THE ONE

Being the ONE is an archetype you must embody as you lead yourself and others. It is also an overarching context for all the other codes. It generously shelters all of who you are: all identities and archetypes. You learn how to embody them as you master your emotional intelligence and navigate with feminine and masculine energy.

Integrating this code for you will make it a robust transmission—setting the ground for all of it. The energy of 'being the one' is the energy of full ownership of your life, like a giant dome on top of the pillars of life.

Understanding the Power of One unwraps two keys. The first is about the compound effect and how to use it. The second is about the profound understanding that you are so lucky, unique, and special to be chosen by yourself as the one born at the right time.

As you read these pages, I want you to step into your "I am the ONE" identity without questioning it. Own it through this code, then live it all within that very truth. The highest frequency is always that of truth. As you align with it, you calibrate to everything you wish for as truth, making the manifestation happen.

The Compound Effect

What you will find unique makes sense because of numbers and how they connect mathematically to energetics, and cracking the different codes is mathematical. It is not only based on physics, but it all makes sense because of numbers and how they mathematically connect. I feel at home when I link everything back to math, exponential schemes, functions, and every other mathematical operation that reflects the intangible world of energetics.

Understanding those scientific aspects will change how you look at your day and life. The compound effect is essential in energetics. Cracking the different codes is how mathematical it is. It is not only based on physics, but it all makes sense because of numbers and how they connect mathematically to remember when bringing wealth and prosperity into your life.

The compound effect summarizes the multiplier effect in alignment with the trend of growth and evolution. Every result we receive starts with one, then more and more. While we all dream of exponential wealth and multiple sources of money, the moment we bring it down to our logic and what we know is the truth around us; it does not feel so true anymore.

Let me show you mathematically how I integrate that truth into my life beyond the notion of time. The numbers will multiply exponentially when we start collapsing time on itself (Codes 9 and 10). Let's say you have a choice today to receive 1 million USD or 1 cent that multiplies daily. Comfort is always our first choice, so it might feel easier to go for the 1 million USD now. But if you remember the compounding effect from your math courses, you can quickly make the first calculation, which shows 1.6 million USD by day 25, when you start with 1 cent, which multiplies daily. The 1.6 million will continue multiplying to very high numbers. This simple operation illustrates how fast comfort-oriented choices may give the type of immediate satisfaction as normalized by the digital era. Nevertheless, taking a moment to step out of the urgency of "needing things right now" will help you see the bigger picture and step out of the time limitation.

The moral of this small calculation is to see how much we sometimes dismiss our results because they feel too little, too slow, and too far from helping us reach our goal in the predicted timeline. We create our pressure and squeeze ourselves into a harmful lack of time attitude.

The compound effect always works by default. It is not something you need to check whether it will work for me or not—there is no need for that. It works because there is no other way. It is what it is. Nevertheless, we will always find a million reasons to stop that compound effect before letting it happen. Often, the choice comes from doubting that it could happen or, worse, from the fear of not being good enough for it all. Instead of trusting the process till the end, we give up.

We stop because it gets too hard to keep the void and that space where there is no evidence of reaching any result. We stop when we are not sure we can handle the void of not knowing, and impatience will make you prefer to choose what does not work rather than waiting.

You need just one good reason to keep believing—just like Lady Gaga's song "Give me one reason for me to stay." To stay in the void, stay believing and lead yourself through the darkness of not knowing from lack of evidence. Your job is to connect with the light of hope, faith and desire.

The one good reason for me was mathematics. I spent many hours, nights, and years studying, grasping the mathematical logic of every operation, problem, and subject I needed to master for my Engineering diploma and then for all the modeling and programming inside my doctorate research. My reason is scientific, which I use in all my teaching. There were moments when I kept going just because my belief was strong, even though I felt like I was inside a long, dark tunnel. I always believed in the light at the end and maintained my focus. My clients' success amplifies my beliefs and my capacity to keep the void and stay focused.

Go Beyond the Fairy Tale Energy

When we break through complex challenges, the first thing that may come to mind is fairy tale stories because they all have many challenges before the happy ending. A prince saved Cinderella because her fairy godmother transformed her into the most beautiful princess in the kingdom. Despite the dark spell, the little mermaid got her voice back when she was with a prince. Or *Beauty and the Beast*, when the beast becomes a beautiful prince after one kiss.

What we know about all these fairy tales is their happiness ever after. But in reality, no one knows what happens afterward. We get to empower ourselves to create that fairy tale frequency. We want that fairy tale frequency of "happy ever after" as our starting point to a greater level.

Instead, we repeat the same cycle or stop at the level of good. You must feel empowered to lead yourself to higher.

The concept of the compound effect adds a constant trend of growth and evolution. It means after the fairy tale, everything you work on will raise you. Every seed you plant will grow. And this continues daily by planting more through your work and connection and doing all the strategic actions you have engineered for yourself. And one day, you will harvest all of them.

Everything is constantly growing. Let's plant tens of seeds a day and water them with love and an energy of hope and positivity. The harvesting season will come around. Flowers will always blossom. When you water the seed Hortensia daily, it will bloom beautifully and colorfully from brown sand. All you need is to trust, hold the vision, and continue improving yourself daily. **Greatness is a compound of excellence, growth, and evolution. It is the moment when you break free and become unstoppable!**

Whatever your journey looks like, don't pull the plug.

Any strategy or plan works. What does not work is stopping and giving up before finishing anything. Even if you finish and are still not to the level you aspire to be, you will have gained momentum and wisdom to reach a higher sphere.

It's time to understand that you need not be successful to feel successful. This phenomenon is one example of the application of the compound effect. But the reality is way different. A lot of times, when someone wants to change jobs, the first thing they do is start losing interest in where they are and what they were supposed to do, putting them in such a low vibration that it will be hard to attract anything better. As you integrate all of these codes, you realize that giving your best and excelling in your service will help you attract what you are meant to do while also feeling fulfilled. Thus, to find a better job, you need to find gratitude for the one you have, even if you don't quite like it. You could connect with the appreciation from your salary, even if it is below what you should receive. You want to compound good things, good vibes, and good emotions. Beware, as the compounding effect works the other way, pulling you towards a vortex of negativity.

You are Meant for Greatness

What you have and see around you becomes the norm in your conscious mind. It becomes a habit and settles in your mind as the comfortable zone. You have worked hard to reach where you are, even though you could have been higher regarding responsibilities, wealth creation, quality of life, and global outreach.

If you feel that what you have is "good" enough, this is for you. We often choose to settle for the "good." The "good" job, the "good" lifestyle, and the "good" daily habits. Then, it all becomes habitually "good."

What if there was more to it? What if you could push yourself to reach your true desires? What if you can open your consciousness and start seeing and feeling how the "extraordinary" could transcend who you are?

When you ask yourself those questions, you become ready to attract more into your life, align with the graceful way of being, and reach the extraordinary.

Everything you do and everything about you will multiply. Your energy will change, and you will become the ONE in charge of your life and everything you attract towards you. You want to build a life based on the desire that you love. So that you can compound with desire, it will make you go to incredible places and reach new heights. It will help you thrive and will make you shine.

We are creating a new lifestyle together. There is no need to struggle anymore to reach success or to get breakthroughs one after the other. All we want is to level from good to great.

The universe is limitless. There is abundance overflowing in multiple dimensions. There is space for everyone; this is when the world needs millions and millions of leaders.

The world needs you for your story, who you are, and what you represent through your voice and spirit. So choose "great". Because as you rise, we all rise!

The Power of "I am the ONE"

At this stage, you are ready to step into the "I am the ONE" identity without questioning it, making an unshakeable decision that your entire life will live inside that truth. This means that you can be anything you want. All you need is to trust yourself and integrate those codes to help you navigate emotions and feelings. Either by untangling things or letting emotions pass when they get too complicated. "I am the ONE" reinforces your trust in yourself when you are hesitant.

This is a severe reclamation for all of us, one to take without extra pressure or stress. Embodying being the ONE helps you wear all your identities as you go through the process of the BAL Method: (1) I am the One to Believe in your inner force, (2) I am the One to Act with the active warrior in you and (3) I am the One to Lead with the attitude of a Boss and the visionary. Being the one is the basis for each identity in every process and every step. It helps balance everything else on top of it.

When you are the ONE, you stop wondering if there is something you may not be able to do. Yes, because you are the one, and you are the only one in the history of the Universe to be who you are, to fulfill your mission, and to turn your dreams into reality.

We often question our worth and abilities, doubting whether we can fulfill our destiny. You were born worthy, and nothing can change that fact. You were born full of potential and possibilities. Often, we get ourselves crushed by the weight of responsibility and the struggles we have experienced in life. Our worthiness never changed.

There are so many examples of people who are doing extraordinary things. The common thread among them is that one day, they have claimed they are the one. Then, they went full on their dream. Artists, scientists, and entrepreneurs all went first, and the universe followed. Nothing will matter until you figure out that you are the ONE and take the leap. Your job today is to do that!

When you let doubt sneak in, you start interacting with a different energy. But when you are the ONE, the first thing you need to do is eradicate all the questioning. You will embody being the ONE. You will use all your power and your authority. It will build your confidence to be all that you are and to do all that you have to do. In addition, when you use your power as the ONE, you will have an incredible relationship with yourself and be able to fulfill your purpose.

Being the ONE doesn't mean circumstances will never shake you because you might have a situation where you didn't honor your word or were unable to do what you expected. It is okay if that identity has taken an extended halt in your life. Just get it back today, even if that break was as long as ten years, 20 years, or even 30 years or more. It's time to wake that identity up again and bring her back!

When you are the ONE, you will walk with all the charisma and magnetism that comes with it, just as if you had sparks of magic moving with your legs. When you are the ONE, your voice will stand out for you. When you are the One, you are extraordinary and constantly growing. You are the one devoted to your mission. When you reconnect with being the ONE, you cannot stop being the one—simply because you are born that way, and it will never go away.

You can create anything when you are the ONE. You can choose to be excellent or dwell in mediocrity. Unfortunately, when you choose the former, it will bring so much authority over your life. The most unfair thing you can do to yourself in all of this is to let life steal life from you.

Get your act together and be the ONE to lead yourself to the best version of yourself. Give yourself full access to the world, make the promise to yourself, and follow through using every one of these codes to witness a progressive growth and evolution trend.

Saying out loud, "I am the ONE," is set to create a tornado of self-fulfilling energy that unleashes the best version of you. Fill your heart with love and compassion, go after your dream, and be grateful for every step you take while keeping your focus on your desire.

Give yourself the promotion and the role you were supposed to carry. Simply because you are genuinely the ONE–and there is nothing that could change that.

Lessons from the Global Mastermind Community

Embodying the ONE as a context for different identities helped Nora, a financial officer in a governmental institution, regain her self-confidence and change what once felt like a toxic environment to becoming recognized as the best team leader and being promoted for it. She could not believe it could ever be possible. Nora started the French program "Femme Leader Experience" as a shy, introverted, brilliant lady dedicated to her up-leveling. Within three months inside our program, she was able not only to boost her confidence but also to appreciate her job daily while starting to take small first actions toward her dream of becoming a successful entrepreneur. She embodied being the ONE to make her dream a reality by strengthening her mindset and taking the first actions to get closer to it.

Be the ONE to Embrace Life with its Duality

You can hold the joy and sadness simultaneously when you are the ONE. You can embrace the beauty of light and the darkness of a volcano's felt vortex. Being the ONE makes you stand in the eye of the storm and rise through its power.

Your role is to train yourself to do it effectively.

When you are the one, you can be both negative and positive. You will still be the one in both emotions and energies. What matters is your actual presence. You cannot be avoidant, nonexistent, or numb. Being the ONE is being the one, no matter what you are going through.

Being the ONE is holding the duality of life with two hands without having them touch and without letting one cover the other: the hardship, the problems, and the struggles in one hand with all the feelings they entail, and the joy, the gratitude, the pride of who you are, the celebrations on the other hand.

What makes you a magnet is your ability to hold both sides together. They go in parallel. They create the polarity that generates electricity, energy, and all vibrations. When people fail, if they stop after the last one, it is considered a failure, but if they do it again, it becomes just a hurdle on the way.

Welcome to the playground of duality, where being solid means holding all of it together: the ups and downs, the successes and failures, the joy and sadness, the ease and struggle. They coexist. You want to navigate through them with all your flowy feminine energy without letting one override the other.

The most powerful lesson I have learned in the field of self-development is how to be sad and happy simultaneously. I have never been able to mix and hold them without pretending to be one or the other. We tend to drop one of them every moment: sadness or happiness.

I just realized how much we pretend. We pretend that we are strong even if our insides are shaky. We pretend to be bubbly even if we don't like it. We pretend that we are happy even if we are sad in reality.

Let go of all of that today. You can feel sad for the many things that have not yet cleared and hold the void with faith and trust. But be happy for all the beauty of life and the potentiality you are so close to having in your hand. Carry both of them without numbing one to let the other take over.

You will love this new way of being. It comes from an energy of truth available in your relationships and work. You will be amazed by all the miracles you create with that energy of truth. Get ready to receive prosperity, wealth, love, and all the world's respect.

Finally, be the ONE to embrace it all and align with the most beautiful frequency of love, joy, wealth, abundance, and peace, with every fiber of your body as the unshakable truth.

ACTIVITY FOR CODE 11

As you embody the identity of Being the One, how will you see yourself in your relationships?

_____
_____
_____
_____
_____
_____
_____
_____

Embody the Identity of Being the One in your Profession. How do you see yourself?

_____
_____
_____
_____
_____
_____
_____

What type of leader will you be when you embody being entirely the ONE?

_____

_____

_____

_____

_____

_____

_____

_____

HAPPINESS

What I have learned in my professional career is the importance of contemplation and taking the time to ground myself. I didn't know about this in the beginning.

Nevertheless, I was intentional about filling my heart with the joy, excitement of the moment, and gratitude for every move I made in my academic years and professional journey. While at Harvard, I walked across the Harvard yard daily, grateful for being there. At the World Bank, I celebrated our incredible impact on changing people's lives. When I worked in the Prime Minister's Cabinet, I was grateful for contributing to national strategies in the high decision-making spheres. Things change later on as entrepreneurs; the responsibilities can get so engulfing that we lose ourselves.

As I contemplate my entrepreneurship journey, I am sure you must do what you love and appreciate—don't choose what you think might work. Any professional journey should be considered fulfillment, betterment, and growth. Taking a moment to appreciate evolution helps you become more intentional and appreciative about every step, bringing gratitude into your routine and feeling the joy around the work and the service you provide.

My drive today is teaching that to hundreds of women worldwide.

Life changes when you start focusing on gratitude and appreciating what you have. Thus, to attract abundance, you want to find yourself in the energetic sphere, navigating through the scale of frequencies. Aligning with the vibration of truth as you connect yourself with your dream objective.

The most minor things will compound and grow to become extraordinary. At this moment, you start understanding how it all happens miraculously!

The path to success we all want to take is one with one foot in gratitude and one foot towards our goals and desires. This way, every step is celebrated in the name of all the gratitude for having it.

Congratulations, this is your last code!

CODE 12
CELEBRATING IN THE NAME OF GRATITUDE

There is sacred wisdom within you,
There are words only you can speak,
There is breath only you can breathe,
There are desires only you are meant to have.

It all exists for you and within you,

Can you show up for all of them, leading with your soul, heart, and truth, feeling the essence of your true self?

Trust everything you hold and carry, and allow it to unfold beautifully. Trust brings magic into your life and the world for all of us.

As you unlock the last of the 12 codes of the Believe Act Lead Sequence, wherever you go next, lead with your truth. Lead with your being and your potency. Tap into your wisdom and feel complete.

This last piece seals this beautiful energy together. It celebrates who you are and the life you are creating for yourself.

My dream is for you to live your life the way you want to tell it as a story and celebrate who you are every step of the way.

A Leader is the Artist and the Game Changer

Leading is an art. There isn't a course you could take or a degree you can receive to make you feel great as a leader. There isn't someone you can copy to grow as a leader. There isn't a user-friendly guide you can follow to get your leadership up and running.

You get to choose to unleash that leader in you or not. You get to decide whether you are the ONE to lead or not. Once you have that first phase under control, you can make your own decision to be or not your leader. Your role is, therefore, to insist on keeping your leadership role no matter what and through the ups and downs of your daily life.

Shape it with your inner creativity, the talent you may have dismissed, and your genius. All of these are what make you unique.

Be the artist and craft your most aligned leadership style. Be a joyful, gorgeous human being and step into the game with your dancing or training shoes—or take your favorite ones with you—and let's do it.

The Game of Leadership

At this stage, you know that everything you want to achieve starts with you leading yourself to create it—whether in your personal or professional life.

There are different ways to do that. There isn't any cookie-cutter toolkit you could plug into to have it automatically done for you. You have to create your toolkit and your model.

I have spent the last four years studying and analyzing human behavior and contemplating what makes leaders stand out and have a happy, fulfilled life and what makes businesses thrive. It is about their approach to leadership and how they feel while taking action.

Leadership is a game you want to learn to play between you and the universe so that you become responsive to what is happening around you. The moment you stop or question things, not only do you waste time, but you lose momentum. And you might quickly find yourself out of the game!

Get back in if you get thrown out for some reason or another. Pick a new uplifted identity and carry on. You want to stay inside the game no matter what you go through and give it all you got. Use your genius, excellence, and agility to do so. Keep the feeling of flow so that you can navigate with the energy of ease and receiving, responding with presence, intentionality, and a power of truth for everything that happens.

Unlocking the Believe Act Lead sequence of the BAL Method helps you integrate the whole process that combines the science of Success, mindset transformation, energetics, and business strategies.

The objective is to play and upgrade your leadership game with all the love, excellence, and empathy you have to create a Masterpiece in your life. Celebrate every step with gratitude, love, and peace.

Leadership is a game in which players must show all their creativity and align with who they are. Only alignment makes you feel true to yourself, so your journey is one of grace, gratitude, and feeling good—a journey that makes you collapse time to make the impossible possible.

Cracking all these codes of self-leadership will elevate you to other spheres of wealth, make you a magnet for beauty and joy, and make you stand out as a leader.

One Step at a Time

When you take time to contemplate your life, you will quickly realize that it's the succession of small things that makes it extraordinary.

Start with the most minor step, the smallest reward, and the smallest action you can take. Nurturing and feeling grateful for it will help you shift away from the feeling of lack.

In the sphere of energetics, it is all about vibration. When you are looking to attract abundance in your life, you need to start from an energy of abundance and never from that of lack.

To project abundance and attract it, you must already feel it emotionally. Filling your heart with gratitude will help you raise your vibrations and settle within the highest thread of love, joy, and abundance.

Let's look at it here from the perspective of time. How could you have any of those feelings when running after time?

It takes a rewiring of how you consider time and appreciate what you do with it. It is also about understanding that success is a journey, not a destination. It is a walk you take. Most importantly, it is about finding the time to pose and anchor in every small step you take. This process is how you will appreciate your walk towards the incredible success you are creating for yourself. The more you enjoy this journey, the more you will be noticed for your excellence and leadership.

The more you can feel grateful for every step you take, the more you will see it compound, attracting more prosperity. Gratefulness is the feeling of receiving and attracting opportunities and abundance. This last code is about celebrating every step in the name of all your gratitude.

Life will Always Give You a Second Chance

Yes, life will always present you with a second chance. Scientifically, it makes sense because there is a perpetual flow of energy. Energy never stops; it is an ever-moving wave of possibilities and potentialities. It continues and never gets destroyed forever, giving you a large blast of luck and opportunities.

The question for you is, how can you see it? Can you grasp it? Can you give yourself the space and the bandwidth to recognize it?

We get a second chance in love, relationships, friendship, business, and leadership.

Naturally, love comes as you become a magnet for appreciation and unconditional love. Love will start showing up in your life differently, like a blast from the past reminding you of what unconditional love felt like as a child, a teenager, and a fresh young soul, or a new encounter from the realm of miracles and fairy tale spirit.

In relationships, it's when you have worked on the standards you want to live by so that you can reinforce all the boundaries around you. Suddenly, every relationship gets redefined with evident respect and consideration.

In friendship, focusing on doing what you love and loving what you do turns you into a magnet for people who want to be around you and feel your vibes. Not because you are the one spending or always pleasing and doing more, but because they just love being around you. They feel increased and seen by your side.

In business, there are millions and millions of new opportunities. When one door gets shut abruptly in front of you, hurting and startling you, do you stay focused entirely on it, feeling inadequate and sorry, wearing the victim costume? Instead, connect with the new energetic space that has opened up for you and fill yourself with something much bigger and better. If you can only surrender to that feeling and hold it as your truth, the seed of hope and possibilities will one day blossom into the most beautiful reality.

When you align with that frequency, you start loving yourself for precisely who you are. Everything will unfold in front of your eyes just like an enchantment.

We live by it inside the BAL Method programs as we create a container to focus on happiness and beauty. We are witnessing so much success from the realm of potentialities and miracles at different levels for each one. I smile and take it all in as the best evidence of how powerful these codes are and how spot-on they are.

All you need is to step outside your bubble and look right and left. See the spark of light you once noticed without seeing it. Follow it. Your heart is the best guidance you could have. Follow it, nurture it with love and faith that everything will work out. Take on the winning attitude by focusing on the beauty of old memories and the new ones you visualize and project into the future. Be ready for all the wisdom from any lesson you grab. They are there to empower you more, strengthen your inner game, and help you rise as a great leader and an inspiring role model.

KEEP SHINING; YOU ARE THE BEACON OF YOUR LIFE!

Be proud of yourself and everything about you.

You are the youngest you can ever be.

Feel beautiful, grand, and empowered to create everything you want.

Remember the incredible human being you are, the one who has gone through all the difficulties. The one who made it despite the odds. The one who spent days and nights finding resilience and courage when you had run out of them.

Remembering yourself is an homage to the incredible human being you are. This last code is for you to remember yourself, to feel the blessing of all you have achieved and all the dreams that make you feel alive. Keep them in your focus and use every fiber of your being to align with them, to magnetize them into your life. You are magic and have all the light you need. It is time to let it shine, for it will make you a beacon in the darkness.

This step isn't just for you. It's for everyone looking for a guide and a story to inspire and carry on.

Peel off every layer of hurt, rage, resentment, deception, guilt, and shame. Lighten up. The time is now to make the change and shine bright like a diamond. You have a mission to fulfill, a legacy to leave behind, and to become that beacon for everyone else. This process can't happen when you carry too much baggage from the past.

FIND YOUR TRUE MISSION AND RISE WITH IT

Find your own mission in line with what you love to do and how you want to serve. When I found mine, it made me feel complete. My mission is about empowering women and young girls to grow confident, resilient, tech-savvy, and financially free while feeling safe and fulfilled. I know how much of this will create ripple effects that will change the world. Because together, we grow.

Together, we rise.

Together, we change the world!

The frequency of us—you, me, and all of us—is the most beautiful one and where magic happens.

I want love, respect, and money for everyone. I want every human to feel, experience, hold, and dive into it wholeheartedly.

It takes so much depth to achieve it.

It is about finding wisdom when it seems impossible. I hold on to the logic inside my mission and my path where no one can see it. I believe in the infinite power and how I could connect with it, elevate myself to become the best version of myself, and guide every woman to unleash the best version of herself.

Self-leadership is what leadership stands on!

INSIDE THE BAL METHOD GLOBAL MASTERMIND COMMUNITY

Celebrating women is my favorite part of all the work we do.

I love watching women succeed. I love seeing them reach new levels of responsibility, leadership, and financial freedom. Nothing is more rewarding than witnessing the changes and being part of the transformational journey.

In the beginning, the first person I celebrated inside the first English Mastermind was Helen from France, who felt stuck, lacking motivation and no inspiration whatsoever. Helen started by joining the Leaders Mastermind and became a private client where we did more focused work together. We followed the process; we integrated every code one by one, and Helen not only was able to finish her PhD thesis with Honors, but she landed a new job, doubling her salary and enjoying every part of it. This celebration was incredible. It provided such a boost of fresh air and brought so much meaning to everything I do. This example confirms the power of readiness to integrate any well-structured self-development program and the importance of our work in changing people's lives.

As I edit this book, I celebrate Afef, who had a beautiful financial career before pursuing her passion for designing and crafting the most beautiful leather-based handbags for elegant women. The moment she started believing in her talent and using her voice to present her unique pieces to the world with the energy of a star, making her masterpieces shine, one of her beautiful pieces was picked by the French Diva Lara Fabian, opening the door to so many possibilities in her life as a global handbag designer.

CELEBRATING WOMEN IS PART OF WOMEN'S EMPOWERMENT

Every year, during March, marketing efforts focus on celebrating women, including National Women's Day. But what happens when the month is over? Do we just go back to forgetting all the work and advances we need to make to empower women worldwide?

No. This ongoing mission calls for a year-long celebration of women for all their responsibilities and the frustration and suffering they have absorbed over the years and past generations.

We want to keep the conversation about women's empowerment alive all year round—a conversation in which women rise, and the world rises with them.

Being a woman is being able to wear several hats at the same time and owning each one of them. Being a woman is being a mum, a daughter, a sister, a friend, a lover, a muse, an artist, a musician, a magician, a healer, a wealth creator, a professional, and a leader. Society expects women to grow up automatically knowing all of those hats somehow. Although there aren't any clear guidelines on how to become all of them at once, every young girl will grow to understand how to use them and change them seamlessly. It took me many years before I fully embodied them as I learned to keep the balance while juggling between them, trusting that each would be okay with every move.

Being prepared and able to carry all these responsibilities takes more than the old paradigm in which we grow up being nice girls. This belief becomes more of a constraint and a limitation for women when they duplicate the same education and guidance they received as young girls.

The world needs a young girl to turn into a great woman. That great woman is on top of her motherhood and sisterhood wounds. She can respect herself and love herself for who she is. A great woman sets standards for herself and others, enforces her boundaries, and earns respect for them. A great woman can lead herself to create the life she aspires to and share love and empathy with the rest of the world.

The world needs women to lead themselves.

Celebrating women is the perfect occasion to share stories about successful women who have paved the way for others and were able to draw all the lessons and find wisdom in everything they have overcome.

When a woman succeeds, she does it for every woman.
When a woman faces a struggle, her story is for every woman.

Celebrating women is not a one-day deal but an everyday way of being. We want to be happy and relieved when we see a woman reaching a high-level leadership position and creating extensive wealth. She shows others what is possible and how every woman can do the same if she chooses to. It is acceptable to prefer to stay comfortable and not go for bigger dreams, while others wish so hard for life to be otherwise.

Additionally, we have another category of those who will feel triggered by other women's successes and start looking for flaws and imperfections to cover their bitter feelings of jealousy and hatred.

We want to build a different world where we respond to each other with love and compassion, where others' successes inspire us, and we wish the best for them the same way we want it for ourselves.

Are we able to do that?

It takes a strong will and the ability for women to lead themselves and to feel inspired by what they encounter in their journey.

It also takes many soft skills to sustain your focus and inspiration. Start with self-love and respect for yourself, mastering your emotional intelligence because leadership means staying intellectually sharp and intelligent while feeling and processing all emotions. And a woman's world is full of emotions!

Women are so similar in their differences.

As women lead themselves, they can create a ripple effect of changes and transformation around them. Leaders influence others by leading themselves first and inspiring others to do the same.

For the world to change, women must empower themselves. We need women to grow confident, resilient, tech-savvy, and financially free. The ripple effect will generate new leaders throughout the world who are outstanding in their field because of their uniqueness and bravery.

The more we are different, the more we are the same in juggling responsibilities and approaching womanhood. Similarities exist in how we approach problems and manage to find a balance.

We should celebrate our similarities, differences, and uniqueness.

The more women succeed from different backgrounds and fields, the more we show everyone the possibilities.

We are grateful for every woman who can stand up for her bravery, her success, and the impact she is making. She is paving the way for others and showing what is possible for her.

Celebrating women is a way to express gratitude for all the incredible women who have pushed the boundaries, raised the standards, and shown what is possible to aim for, aspire to, and create in your life.

And you want to do the same for yourself, expanding abundance.

Be grateful for every step you make, and celebrate yourself every day!

Let's Have It All, Shall We?

Congratulations on taking the time to go through this whole book and crack the codes one after the other.

You have mastered the whole sequence of Believe Act Lead in a way that makes you accelerate its integration to become your way of being and enhance your leadership style.

I want you to sit up and feel ready for what is coming next and prepared to take on the world. So much fascination awaits if you just surrender to it and its elevating power. When you hit this emotion in your body, you will find something incredible and start creating a symbiosis with the universe, like a perfect dance responding to every move from the universe with grace and alignment.

There is a masculine-driven way to succeed and a feminine-energy way. Unlocking these codes will open a new season with more love, joy, happiness, fulfillment, and peace of mind. Learning to play with emotions and energetics will align you with different objectives, from respect, appreciation, and wealth to reaching higher levels in the leadership sphere.

In the same way we let our childhood trauma tarnish our lives, we need to allow our childhood joy to take over when we need it to. We attach it to receiving money and anything we deeply desire. We bring stress and fear into any equation until it starts altering our worthiness and robbing the beauty of life out of our own lives.

There is an even higher frequency for money and prosperity, which is that of magnetizing magic money. When there is so much magic money, it will take care of all the rest, covering all the debt and all the needs. The compound effect will make it grow so much more.

To set the stage for this, you can start visualizing many beautiful childhood memories and happy ones about money, such as waking up and finding money under the pillow after the tooth fairy took your tooth and replaced it or a relative giving you cash in an envelope for your birthday. My favorite is finding unexpected money in a handbag you have left untouched for weeks or months. All of this makes you giggle when you think about it. Magic money feels good and happy. Visualizing should become part of your routine when manifesting cash and prosperity.

Money is the new layer added to the BAL Method with this sequence of codes—a whole set of modules to work on understanding exponential wealth and the energetics of money and currency. Rewriting your story with money is essential to magnetizing wealth and abundance in our hands for ourselves and the world.

IT's TIME TO CELEBRATE YOU

Celebration is the most essential part of success. This code changes your perspective about leading yourself through your life to create a Masterpiece and build an incredible legacy!

When you crack through this code, it will become a source of joy in your life and the lives of everyone who comes closer to you and your work.

We go through many things in life that feel like déjà-vu or patterns repeating themselves to create the same cycle over and over again. We think something is wrong with us and start dwelling in a negative direction. It could be related to money, relationships, or your job. Nothing is wrong with you; it is just a pull to learn another level and move on.

Life is about growth and evolution, and we are cyclical beings. Things we go through will always come back, but we conquer them better and better each time: losses, bankruptcy, heartbreaks. We grow stronger, more equipped, and wiser each time. Even though it feels like we are going backward, it is only an illusion due to all the emotions that get us triggered. They make us forget what we are capable of.

Any direction and any trend needs the anchoring of each step. If we don't take the moment to anchor every advancement we make, they vanish as if they never existed. And we find ourselves on a hamster wheel, living the same things repeatedly. For every small step and every tiny leap, even if it is barely overcoming a situation, you need a moment to breathe and fill your heart with gratitude. Celebration is about anchoring every move forward with revelry in the name of gratitude. It could be as small as treating yourself to a bath, a delicious hot chocolate, or a meal with loved ones, friends, or just by yourself.

You will love this concept so much when you apply it. It changes everything. You will get so busy celebrating and stacking so many small achievements, one on top of the other. Particularly the one you usually ignore for being too little or too far from what you want to reach.

This code is everything we want to be when it comes to falling in love with your life and creating a life of joy. You start romanticizing your very existence.

I was very intentional about it as it became a central piece in my daily life and work. My appreciation for my work grew immensely when I started celebrating women making great leaps and changing their lives. The celebrations were so diverse and beautiful. We celebrated women falling in love with their lives again and finding a sense of living after a setback, bankruptcy, or rejection.

Celebrate even reading this very book till the end.

Please don't despair. Your circumstances do not exist to break or destroy you. The universe throws some challenging events to help us change our path. It is difficult to see when we feel overwhelmed, worried, stuck, or untangled in habits we can't break free from. The wake-up call can be harrowing at times.

Now I love my work for all the celebrations.

I love my work for all the gratitude I record every morning.

I love my work for the purity of love; it magnetizes into my life and those who come close to me.

I celebrate, and I want you to do the same!

Celebrate every move, every step, everything you do. Do it in the name of gratitude. In the name of all the emotions of feeling 'Yes I did,' 'Yes I am alive,' 'Yes I am in charge.'

Celebrate when you realize you are the ONE. Celebrate when you learn your mantra by heart by creating your extraordinary cheerleading voice. Celebrate when you become intentional about yourself.

Make every celebration a party thrown in the name of gratitude.

Hype and Excitement

We often get the energy confused between excitement and gratitude. These are two different things, vibrating on various levels.

When we get close to achieving a goal, there is a moment when it is almost there, and we feel all the excitement that comes with it. That closeness, that feeling of almost being there, creates a big hype. Then, when we reach the very goal we worked so hard for and waited so long for, we don't feel that much excitement anymore. We have a disappointing moment. It feels like, okay, now what else?

We then get ourselves all ready for the next goal—and the cycle keeps repeating itself.

The excitement fades away. The hype builds up because of the illusion and the excitement—and then it disappears. For example, parties are usually thrown before something big happens, like New Year's Eve. A big moment is the countdown from 12 to 0 just before midnight, which gets everyone in such a hype and a state of excitement. It is incredibly contagious and intoxicating.

Right after that, the whole hype and excitement story fades away. We become indifferent. We love celebrating the first anniversaries of a relationship or the first month in a new, exciting job. We celebrate more years–the second and third—and then the excitement dwindles. After a while, we cannot keep track of the number of years so quickly.

That said, the celebration we discuss here is about something other than excitement. It is an anchoring of your journey with gratitude for all the time and years spent together if it is an anniversary. It is a moment of recognition for all your courage and ability to learn, grow, and elevate to a better version of yourself. The gratitude changes it all, bringing a lasting feeling and something that makes you feel ready to celebrate.

ALIGN WITH THE FREQUENCY OF MAGIC

The frequency of magic is that of celebration. And there is so much magic we should become available for from whatever source it may come.

Don't we just love those types of frequencies?

Created from the gratitude for who we are, these frequencies give us hope and a new sense of life. The more we align with them, the more they compound.

We stop celebrating when we get overwhelmed with problems and let negativity take over our lives. We stop celebrating because we are humble, discreet, or too worried about what others will say. We also stop celebrating because we feel guilty. In reality, what we do is desensitize our success.

But when it comes from a space of gratitude, it holds an energy of sharing, inspiring, and showing others what is possible. And we all need more proof that it is possible to elevate, create wealth, succeed, and rewrite your story.

One reason self-development is essential is that we all want to have a life that feels fulfilling and prestigious. We want to find meaning in what we do.

The desire to find meaning is why these twelve codes are transformative. They help you get excited again about all the possibilities and step into the field of potentiality and miracles. You learn to understand your power and master your emotional intelligence.

Your job is to anchor yourself in gratitude even if you are still in the middle of the storm or buried under a lot of heaviness. Embracing the duality of life is feeling grateful and finding the minor ways to celebrate it, even disciplining your mind to think of hope and that "everything is going to be okay" despite the storm.

Whatever you undertake, do it in the name of appreciation. Anchor it in and celebrate that you are grateful for it. This action will trigger an up-leveling to an energetic frequency that will magnetize opportunities and beauty into your life to be more thankful about. Most importantly, it helps you keep the joy alive and align with more of it.

Finally, celebrate your real feelings by sharing the truth from your heart and soul. Sharing our milestones and journey from a place of truth and recognition feels aligned, like a transfer of codes and calibration keys. It is sharing a light of hope and potentiality. It is the greatest gift you can give yourself and offer the world.

It is worth celebrating.

This is Your Time to Shine

The world needs a leader precisely like you.
    Don't hide; don't shrink yourself to fit a mold.

Spread your wings and rise like a phoenix.
    Fly to the highest frequencies of magic.
    Let your colors show, be appreciated, and be loved.

Let the beauty of your work and your heart blow your mind.
    Celebrate who you are in the name of gratitude.
    Give yourself a standing ovation for every milestone.

You are beautiful, intelligent, unique, extraordinary, and worthy of every desire and every dream you have inside.

Go on and make it your reality!

With love, light, gratitude, respect, and wonder,
    Dr. Hynd

ACTIVITY FOR CODE 12

Rewrite your dream goals and postulate their potentiality into the universe.

Hold the vibe for them so they become the truth in your eyes.

Be grateful for every step you take.

Celebrate every milestone, no matter how small it seems compared to your bigger dream, and anchor it so you can start aligning to the frequency of Magic.

What are you celebrating today?

What have you done to get closer to your objective?

Even reading this book, understanding every Code and integrating your new lifestyle is to be celebrated.

Be proud of yourself and find three things you want to celebrate in your personal life, professional life and self-development.

_____

_____

_____

FOUR YEARS INTO MY STORY

It has been four years since my business scrambled and became a public embarrassment. Today, as I put on my navy suit with a white chiffon shirt, I found myself back at that same place for a meeting and thought to myself.

What If I had waited for things to be fixed and to return to normal all these years?

What if I had waited for validation from outside and for circumstances to return as they were?

That would be four years of doing nothing, just hanging on to the past and waiting for things to return. Four years wasted instead of being and feeling alive. Four years of losing it slowly to depression. But I didn't!

Today, I am proud of the woman in me who believed in love and resilience and kept them combined all the way.
I am proud of the woman in me who understood the duality of life and what forgiveness meant.
I am proud of the woman I became during those four years.

I am proud of the woman who received coaching, mentoring, and all the psychological help she needed.
I am proud of understanding inner power and becoming disciplined to embody it fully.
I am proud of the BAL Method I created on the way.
I am proud of these 12 Codes we get to crack together here.
I am so proud of all the other women and men I was able to uplift along with me,
I am so proud of the success they have created in their business,
I am so proud of the joy they brought to their lives and families.

Could I have done this if I just pushed the 'pause on image' button and stayed stuck there—waiting for a miracle to land on my lap?

NEVER in a million years.

Failure is part of your path. Success can never happen at a high level if you don't fall and stand back up. Success is about recreating yourself, defining a new paradigm, strengthening your faith, embodying a different identity, and understanding that the universe brings what you need on your path to give you the lessons and the wisdom to carry on into another sphere of elevation.

Let this be your sign to see love and gratitude in who you are.
    Let this be your sign to find something in you to be proud of.
    Let this be your sign to be the one creating magic and miracles!

The World needs you for who you are –make every minute count.
    You owe it to yourself!

Thank You

If you have enjoyed or found value in this book, please take a moment to leave an honest/brief review on <u>Amazon</u> or <u>Goodreads</u> . Your reviews help prospective readers decide if this is right for them & it is the greatest kindness you can offer the author.

Thank you in advance.

QR CODE— forthcoming

ABOUT THE AUTHOR

Dr. Hynd Bouhia is a mother of four, an entrepreneur, a strategist, and a leadership mentor.

Dr. Hynd has accumulated over 25 years of professional experience in high-level leadership positions in strategy and finance. Forbes nominated her among the 100 most influential Arab women in Business (2015) and honored her as a member of the Johns Hopkins Society of Scholars (2018).

With a Harvard PhD in environmental engineering and sustainable development and an Engineering degree from Centrale Paris, Dr. Hynd started her career at the World Bank in Washington, working on development projects and infrastructure. She then joined Morocco's Prime Minister as an economic advisor, working on elaborating Morocco's industrial strategies and structuring large-scale investment projects in industry, energy, and tourism. Dr. Hynd was appointed the Managing Director of the Casablanca Stock Exchange and structured and managed several investment funds before launching the consulting firm Strategica, which specialized in economic intelligence, strategic consulting, and impact entrepreneurship.

Dr. Hynd is the author of the Bestseller Believe Act Lead: Your Journey to Success, Wealth, and Making an Impact. She is also the author of two inspirational women's empowerment books: *Africa Girl, African Woman: How Agile, Empowered, and Tech-savvy Females Will Transform the Continent...for Good* and the French book *Filles et Femmes du Monde Moderne: comment Deviennent-elles Leaders du continent*.

Dr. Hynd founded the BAL Method, focusing on leadership, self-development, and mentorship. It offers several digital courses, group programs in a Mastermind setting, and a private, exclusive circle.

https://www.facebook.com/groups/212127987771543

Register here for the free masterclass:
www.balmethod.com/bal

Join our Leaders Mastermind
www.balmethod.com/leadersmastermind

instagram.com/hyndbouhia
linkedin.com/in/hynd-bouhia-phd-0289a3a3

ALSO BY DR. HYND BOUHIA

Believe Act Lead: Your Journey to Success, Wealth and Making an Impact

https://www.amazon.com/dp/1955683220

―――

Africa Girl, Africa Woman: *how agile, empowered and tech-savvy female will transform the continent...for good*

https://www.amazon.com/gp/product/B08Z8FQ6H5

―――

Filles et femmes de l'Afrique Moderne: comment deviennent-elles des leaders du continent

https://www.amazon.com/gp/product/B091P9WK2F

―――

Water in the Macroeconomy: International water in the national planning

https://www.amazon.com/gp/product/B07CQ146QM

RED THREAD PUBLISHING

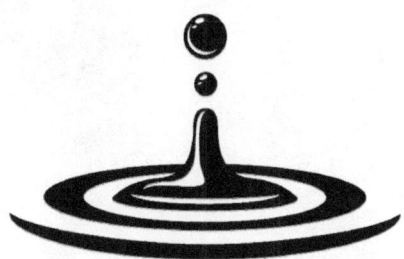

Red Thread Publishing is an all-female publishing company on a mission to support 10,000 women to become successful published authorpreneurs & thought leaders.

To work with us or connect regarding any of our growing library of books email us at **info@redthreadbooks.com.**

To learn more bout us visit our website **www.redthreadbooks.com.**

Follow us & join the community.

facebook.com/redthreadpublishing

instagram.com/redthreadbooks